Reimagining Malcolm X

Street Thinker versus Homo Academicus

Seyed Javad Miri

University Press of America,® Inc.
Lanham • Boulder • New York • Toronto • Plymouth, UK

Copyright © 2016 by University Press of America,® Inc.
4501 Forbes Boulevard, Suite 200, Lanham, Maryland 20706
UPA Acquisitions Department (301) 459-3366

Unit A, Whitacre Mews, 26-34 Stannary Street,
London SE11 4AB, United Kingdom

All rights reserved
Printed in the United States of America
British Library Cataloguing in Publication Information Available

Library of Congress Control Number: 2015939298
ISBN: 978-0-7618-6607-7 (pbk : alk. paper)

"Excerpts from MALCOLM X SPEAKS, copyright © 1965 by Merit Publishing and Betty Shabazz. Used by permission of Grove/Atlantic, Inc. Any third party use of this material, outside of this publication, is prohibited."

∞™ The paper used in this publication meets the minimum requirements of American National Standard for Information Sciences Permanence of Paper for Printed Library Materials, ANSI/NISO Z39.48-1992.

Contents

Prologue		v
Note		xiii
Introduction		1
1	Novel Strategies of Interpretation	9
	Novel Reading Strategies	9
	Uniform Strategies of Reading	11
	House Negro and Field Negro	11
	Academic Form of Analysis	15
	Note	17
2	Undisciplinary Fields of Knowledge	19
	Descartes versus Rumi	19
	Tutelage and the Riddle of Subjectivity	22
	Symbolism Unthought	25
	Field Strategies of Resistance	26
	Note	30
3	Violence, Religion, and Extremism	31
	Militant Secularism and Fanatic Religionism	31
	Racial Revolution	35
	Historiography of Revolt/Revolution in Sociology	40

	Revolution and Radical Means of Political Transformation	45
4	The Epic of America	53
	The Mystery of Unsaid	53
	Racism and American Foreign Policy	56
	Islam, Religion, and the Question of Hermeneutics	57
	Good Society	65
	The Prophetic and the Analytic	69
	Academia and the Prophetic Perspective	73
	Personal Scholarly Narrative	75
Epilogue		79
References		83

Prologue

The death of Michael Brown, 18, on August 9 in 2014 will be a turning point in the history of America, in general, and in the collective memory of Black community, in particular. Why should this date be considered as a defining moment in the future history of America? Before answering this question, it is necessary to elaborate on this issue and then move to analysis of this incident which forced the black president of the United States of America to order Jay Nixon who is the governor of Missouri to use the National Guard in a limited fashion by urging that healing should be the overall policy rather than violence. Missouri's governor imposed curfew for the St. Louis suburb of Ferguson.

The official narrative was constructed in a fashion that the deployment of the National Guard troops were due to days of violent unrest which resulted in looting and burning of stores in this part of America. In other words, the system is construing a story to show that the problem is a simple incident which has nothing to do with the question of legitimacy. But the slogans of the protestors demonstrate a different picture as what they perceive as the core problem is not one policeman's individual act of murdering an American citizen. On the contrary, while they were marching in a slow loop along a stretch of downtown Ferguson, they were pounding drums and chanting *the whole damn system is guilty as hell*. Here there are several elements which make up a grim picture of the future of race relations in America and wherever the demarcation of social relations is based upon the concept of "race" rather than "humanity." To put it differently, this incident shows to black people in America once again that even when the president is a black man the problem in race-stricken society would not change in fundamental fashion due to the fact that race is not a personal question but a social question which shapes the mode of *americanness* in its widest sense of the term.

This is to argue that the race problem cannot solely be removed by quotas policy without taking into consideration the existential dimensions of racism which has deeply entered the subconscious of the white elites in the United States of America. On the other hand, the position of President Obama is interesting sociologically as it demonstrates that the modern state is not a democratic institution by essence but by accident. In other words, even the most democratic defender of democracy in the world when it is faced with cultural issues it has no other option but the deployment of brute force.

In addition, it is clear that Obama is openly confessing that the governor of Missouri should use "violence" to extinguish the fire of systematic racism which has created a deep sense of injury in the hearts of black people as a community. This is to argue that even the most powerful state on the earth is still a "Leviathan State" rather than a liberal (in the sense of emancipative institution at the service of humanity). When President Obama urges Jay Nixon that "healing" should be the policy but at the same time permits the use of violence against black people this shows clearly that there is a paradox which has not been solved since the assassination of Malcolm X. He believed that in America there is a deep-rooted problem which he conceptualized it as the *cancer of racism*. There have been many different strategies in removing this cancer in America but the August 9 turning-point demonstrates clearly that the cancer is still with us and shall not be removed by military force.

How could this problem be solved? If you ask the scholars on race in Europe or America such as Steve Fenton they would not answer you in an existential fashion. The problem of race is constructed as a social problem without taking into consideration its importance as a belief-system which persists in postmodern societies of Europe and America. In other words, the question which needs to be addressed is race as a belief-system which persists in the heart of certain group of people who seem to have authority over other weaker groups in various societies.

To my knowledge, no social theorist has looked at this question better than Malcolm X as he did not look at racism as a social problem which needs to be addressed solely in terms of sound social policy. On the contrary, he believed that the American society is infected by a cancer and the body is in deep pain. In other words, it seems Obama has subconsciously reflected what Malcolm X had envisaged half a century ago (April 20, 1964) in Mecca where he pondered upon racism in America. Obama in his talk with Jay Nixon used the term "healing" and Malcolm 50 years ago used the term "cancer" when thinking about racism in America and both these terms refer to a body which is in a terrible shape and in dire need of attention. But the question is how to attend a cancerous body which is taking day by day the power of the body of society away in a drastic fashion. This is the question which Malcolm X thought about when he was in Mecca in April 20, 1964. In his view,

> America needs to understand Islam, because this is the one religion that erases the race problem from its society. Throughout my travels . . . I have met, talked to, and even eaten with, people who would have been considered *white* in America, but the religion of Islam in their hearts has removed the *white* from their minds. They practice sincere and true brotherhood with other people irrespective of their color (1966. 59–60).

In other words, the problem of racism cannot be solved through political trickeries if those who are supposed to be under the spell of politics do not remove the racial consciousness from their minds and hearts. This is to argue that racism is incompatible with modernity and we cannot found modern institutions on archaic notions. Malcolm X believed that America would be destroyed unless she changed the philosophical foundations of herself which is deeply intertwined with racism. He argued that before

> America allows herself to be destroyed by the *cancer of racism* she should become better acquainted with the religious philosophy of Islam, a religion that has already molded people of all colors into one vast family, a nation or a brotherhood of Islam that leaps over all *obstacles* and stretches itself into almost all the Eastern countries of this earth (1966. 60).

Of course, it may be hard to accept this view today when Islam has been portrayed as a religion of violence but the notion of religion in Malcolm X's view is not of an exclusivist nature. On the contrary, Malcolm X seems to hold a dialogical notion of religion which embraces all members of different congregations under the same umbrella of divine prophetic tradition.

Today Malcolm X is not among us anymore but his words echo through the labyrinths of time in a clear fashion and urging all philosophers and social theorists to realize that racism is a problem; racism is a cancer; racism cannot be removed through legislation; and racism is a belief-system. In other words, if one agrees that racism is a belief-system then you cannot remove a belief by resorting to legislation as belief is rooted in the hearts and minds of people in a profound fashion.

Malcolm X believed that the cancer of racism has the ability to destroy America in the same fashion that racism by Hitler brought destruction upon Germans. In the end of his *Meccan Epistle* he wrote, you may be

Shocked by these words coming from me, but I have always been a man who tries to face facts, and to accept the reality of life as new experiences and knowledge unfold it. The experiences of this pilgrimage have taught me much, and each hour here in the Holy Land opens my eyes even more. If Islam can place the spirit of true brotherhood in the hearts of the *whites* whom I have met here in the Land of the Prophets, then surely it can also remove the *cancer of racism* from the heart of the white American, and perhaps in time to save America from imminent racial disaster, the same destruction brought upon Hitler by his racism that eventually destroyed the Germans themselves (1966. 60).

In other words, the recent killing and then demonization of an unarmed 18-year-old Afro-American youth, Michael Brown, in Ferguson, Missouri by a white police officer has made visible how the *cancer of racism* is still a dominant part and parcel of the neoliberal American capitalism. This is to argue that it is a mistake to simply focus on the militarization of the police and their racist actions in addressing the killing of Michael Brown. What we are witnessing in this brutal butchery and mobilization of state violence is symptomatic of the neoliberal, racist, punishing state, with its encroaching machinery of social death. To put it differently, the cancer of racism has developed into a multifaceted dragon which cannot tolerate any sense of aspiration in the public square. This is to argue that "worldwide capitalism can no longer sustain or tolerate . . . global equality. It is just too much" (Žižek, 2013. 58). Moreover, in the face of institutionalized racism, massive inequality, increasing poverty, the rise of the punishing state, and the attack on all public spheres, cancerous racist neo-liberalism can no longer pass itself off as synonymous with democracy. Here we are faced with new forms of realities which are not grounded in any sense of humanistic metaphysics and the result of these diverse forms of inhumanities is what Malcolm X envisaged as "cancer" in the body of human society, in general, and "cancer of racism" in the body of American society, in particular. In this work, I have attempted to revisit Malcolm X in terms of his social theory and see if we can form concepts of sociological relevance in an alternative set of theoretical endeavours.

The idea of this book grew out of a discussion which I had with my American friend and colleague, i.e. Professor Dustin J. Byrd from Oliver College in United States of America in 2011. As the editor of Islamic Perspective, I had the honour to receive a review article by Professor Byrd on Malcolm X, which was related to Manning Marable's controversial biography of Malcolm X. I published that book review in the Journal of Islamic Perspective in Volume 6, 2011. However during 2011 to 2013 our discussions became more serious and I proposed a book project on Malcolm X and to this proposal, Professor Byrd graciously replied in the following fashion,

> I do think we should think about a book/project on Malcolm X. There has been a renaissance concerning Malcolm since the publishing of Dr. Manning Marable's book *Malcolm X: A Life of Reinvention*. This book has stirred a lot of controversy concerning Malcolm's private life. However, what is severely lacking in the discussion is Malcolm's Islamic faith. Most in the U.S. remember him as a *Black Nationalist , separatist , left-revolutionary*, but not as a Muslim. This may be the angle we should explore as well as him being a bridge between the Muslim world and others in the U.S. Nevertheless, Malcolm needs to be remembered and studied both here and in the Muslim world. We definitely should embark on that project (Byrd, 2013).[1]

The project which we talked about grew into a book with many contributors from different scholars who came from various countries such as US, Singapore, Iran and Turkey. The book is planned to be published in 2015 in the fiftieth anniversary of Malcolm X's assassination. For that project, I worked upon the *Meccan Epistle* and tried to revisit the legacy of Malcolm X in the light of present dilemmas in the extremist climate of international arena. However, while I was working on this project I realized that there are few works on Malcolm X as a social theorist. In other words, I came only across few articles or papers where one could find scant references to him as a social thinker or a social theorist. I searched for him in sociological journals but more I looked for less I could find anything on Malcolm X as an important figure within sociological discourses. This complete silence on him reminded me of a passage in Dustin J. Byrd's review article in *Islamic Perspective* where he asks a very significant question about Malcolm X, i.e. why was Al-Hajj Malik al-Shabbazz more of a threat than Malcolm X? (Byrd, 2011. 251). The answer given by Byrd is very important for those who are looking for Malcolm X's shift from "a limited 'Black' struggle to struggle of the oppressed against the oppressor" (Byrd, 2011. 256–7). However, the inspiration that I got from Byrd's question led me to ask another type of question, i.e. why is Malcolm X absent in global sociological discourses? His key concepts of "house negro" and "filed negro" could be employed in various post-western studies on culture, personality, subjectivity and authenticity. In post-colonial studies on film, art, cinema, literature, social theory we can use Malcolm X's key concepts but the truth is that there are no studies either on Malcolm X or through Malcolmian theories and concepts. I remember in early stages of this book in 2013 I spoke about Malcolm X to the President of Iranian Sociological Association (Professor S. Mohammad Amin Ghaneirad) who is my good friend and colleague and he was not thrilled about the idea. But when I explained the key concepts of Malcolm X on house mentalité versus field mentalité he found them very interesting and thrilling. In other words, it seems even the restern social theorists are not very familiar with possible contributions of alternative social thinkers such as Malcolm X. To put it differently, I think the Malcolm X studies have just begun and as my good friend Dustin J Byrd has told, we are experiencing a kind of renaissance as far as Malcolm X is concerned. We need to look at intellectual dimensions of Malcolm X's social thought and philosophy as they are very badly undertheorized. There are certain good colleagues of mine here in Iran who argue that it is better to leave studies on Malcolm X to American scholars who are better equipped to carry on the good research. For instance, my good colleague and friend Professor Seyed Buik Mohammadi believes that Malcolm X has been studied by American scholars in better fashion and there is no need for us in Iran to look at Malcolm X independently. In other words, we should read him within parameters of American strategies of scholarship as they have conceptualized him in a more advanced fashion. Although I think he has a point here but it is very naive to think that we should think only in local terms and leave the global issues to others as though there is a division of labour in the world of scholarship. Instead of thinking of the world of scholarship in terms of "division of labour" we should conceptualize it in terms of "perspective." This is to argue, issues within humanities and the world of humanity could be better understood in terms of one's position in existential sense rather than demarcating problems in terms of division of labour. On the other hand, there are personalities in the human history that could play the role of bridges between cultures and nations during critical moments in the history of mankind. I think, Malcolm X could be one of these rare intellectuals who could be employed as a bridge between Iran and America where the public squares of these respective countries have become very sensitive toward each other after 4 decades of animosities. Seen in this fashion, then we cannot leave Malcolm X only to American scholars and researchers as they may not be interested in him in terms of a significant medium of dialogue between the two countries. In other words, the types of studies which scholars would carry in America would surely differ from the kinds of studies which Iranian scholars may embark upon due to the simple fact of perspective which plays an important role in the constitution of scholarship in humanities and cultural studies.

NOTE

1. A private talk with Professor Dustin J. Byrd in 25th March 2013.

Introduction

Every social theory is based on a philosophy and any philosophy is founded upon a metaphysical vision of reality—which, in turn, springs out of a deep concern/care about the fundamental nature of life. In other words, the total endeavors of self in the matrix of life brings this naked question before human soul (or what we term lexically as "I") that what is the end of this sojourn which seems to be inexplicable? Concern or *Sorge* plays a significant role in Heidegger's philosophy as it is *Sorge* that signifies a human being's existence and makes it meaningful. To be-in-the-world in an authentic existential pretext is to be *careful*. Heidegger concluded that "care" is the primordial state of *Being* as *Dasein* strives towards authenticity (Steiner, 1978). When your primordial state is intertwined with carefulness in its most authentic fashion then contextual reality which is actualized in all possible alienating forms of carelessness such as exploitation, degradation, oppression, denial of the *other*, and enslavement of the *other* then a sense of rage may express itself. This *rage* may primarily be expressed in a personal level but when the roots of rage are not only confined to the boundaries of an individual life but, as a matter of fact, it is the salient characteristic of collective existence then the rage may take different shapes and forms. Although care is a fundamental mode of being but rage is as essential as *sorge* whenever the totality of being is denied based on accidental indices which do not play significant role in the constitution of self and society. The rage could be an expression that one's total being has been conditioned upon the mode of life which is not designed in accordance to "my own being." Heidegger puts this in an interesting fashion by arguing that the world into which our Dasein is thrown has others in it, and the existence of others is totally indispensable to its facticity of Being-there. Understanding of others in the world and the association of the ontological status of others with our own Dasein is, in itself, a form of *Being*, i.e. *Being-in-the-world* is a being-with, and that the understanding of the presentness of others is to exist. However, being-with presents the possibility of comprehending our own Dasein as an everyday Being-with-one-another where we may come to exist not on our own terms, but only in reference to others. In so doing, we eventually come to not be ourselves, and surrender our existence to a formless "Theyness" or alterity (Steiner, 1978). This is to argue that the "belonging to others" is a drastic irresponsibility because the "they" deprives the particular Dasein of its own accountability by making every decision and judgment for it. The "they" can do this most easily because it can always be said that "they" were responsible for such and such. Heidegger said that this passivity creates the alienated self, the "Man" who is fatally disburdened of moral autonomy and, therefore, of moral responsibility. This "Man" can know no ethical guilt. Heidegger called this the "self of everyday Dasein" or the "they-self," the total opposite of the solid singularity of a Dasein which has grasped itself. This crucial distinction was important for Heidegger as it is the distinction between an authentic and an inauthentic human existence (Steiner, 1978). But this inauthenticity does not create within itself a sense of rage as one does not have any self-consciousness about the nature of one's own dependency. If one has been forced into factual dependency (e.g. slavery) then the context of reflection may dramatically differ as it did for Malcolm X in a post-slavery but racially-constructed system in America which forced the black community into an eternal state of alterity.

If it is agreed that the inauthentic human person does not live as itself but as "they" live, then how would one understand the enslaved person who is not even living the inauthentic life? In other words, the racial state of America during Malcolm X's life created a climate for black people to be able to realize the angst in their every bones and guts. Existentialist philosophers argue that angst is one of the primary instruments through which the ontic character and context of everyday existence is made inescapably aware of, is rendered naked to, the pressures of the ontological. And further, angst is a mark of authenticity, of the repudiation of the "theyness" (Warnock, 1970).

The repudiation of the white supremacy in the discourse of Malcolm X has been wrongly understood as a criminal act against the security of the United States of America during the turbulent years of the Cold War era. Some even argued that his radicalism was a sign of inferiority which he felt before other distinguished leaders of the Civil Rights Movement. But these theories do not explain the intellectual brilliance of Malcolm X's key concepts of "Field-Negro" and "House-Negro" which could be loosely correlated to the key concepts of authentic and inauthentic being in existentialist philosophies of the 20th century. In other words, the radicalism of Malcolm X was a progressive way of repudiating the "they-life" which overshadowed all aspects of the black people (and by extension all the colonized and westernized people around the globe) who seemed unable to distinguish between authentic and inauthentic lives.

The first question which may come to mind is that why should a sociologist care about Malcolm X? In other words, in what sense is Malcolm X of importance in the field of sociological studies? To answer this question, one needs to define sociology as it may mean differently to different scholars in different theoretical paradigms. For instance, in eurocentric paradigms there would be no room for a thinker such as Malcolm X as a sociologist within eurocentric frameworks should submit to disciplinary principles which have been erected by institutionally-oriented professionals at various departments of social sciences around the globe. In this sense, we should rest assured that Malcolm X is not a sociologist or even a social theorist which is a broader concept than sociology. For instance, the approach taken by Anthony Giddens is an excellent example of eurocentric interpretation of sociological imagination when he mentions a highly acclaimed thinker such as Ivan Illich. In Giddensian approach, Illich does not qualify to be a sociologist or social theorist due to the fact that he does not have a disciplinary approach to human lifeworld. Illich does occupy only a footnote in Giddensian vision of social theory. But it is not hard to realize that the Giddensian approach is not equivalent to sociological imagination as such but a partisan usurpation of lifeworld imagination. In other words, Giddens has taken the eurocentric imagination of lifeworld tantamount to universal imagination of human world. Said differently, Malcolm X is of significance for theoretical endeavors for those who aspire to transcend eurocentric vision of reality and construct alternative modes of conceptualizations. But before getting into theoretical debates and conceptual engagements we need to focus on misconceptions which exist around and about Malcolm X. For example, the common mistake about Malcolm X is that he *"was primarily a speaker, not a writer. The only things . . . written by him are his memorandum to the Organization of African Unity in Cairo and some letters"* (Breitman in Malcolm X, 1966. Viii). I would like to go even further and argue that the more detrimental mistake is that scholars believe that he should not be considered as a social theorist because he has not written anything worth considering in regard to social theory. Of course, I should admit that sociologists and social theorists in Europe and USA are better equipped as far as Malcolm X is concerned as they have started to change their positivistic verdicts on theorists outside the canon but the same I cannot tell about the restern sociologists, in general, and Iranian sociologists, in particular. In Iran, there is no debate on Malcolm X as a writer, as a thinker and not at all as a social theorist of higher caliber. When talking to colleagues about the significance of Malcolm X at sociological association in Iran, I was questioned about the validity of this research. To be honest, few even knew about his works and theories in post-colonial discourses along with Fanon, Shariati, Spivak, Chakrabarty, and Said. In Iran, American history is conceptualized in White terms and there is no color awareness which dominates the historiographical parameters of the American story. In other words, scholars and common people in Iran have internalized the American history in White fashions and there is no debate on whether one could read the American Dream in a different mode than the mainstream approaches which are taught through textbooks which are again written by White mentality. To put it differently, the American historiography is written in a fashion that brings to mind Hebrew Hagiography, i.e. a sanctification of the Founding Fathers or Pilgrims. But Malcolm X presents a different narrative on the American history. He argues that *Negroes* were *"brought here by the people who came here on the Mayflower, [they] . . . were brought here by the so-called pilgrims . . . or Founding Fathers"* (Breitman in Malcolm X, 1966. 5).

This is to argue that the emergence of America is intertwined with oppression of a great part of humanity, i.e. Negros; this provides us a different story about American historiography. But the view of Malcolm X which is full of innovative notions and it could, as a matter of fact, provide us with alternative vector is absent in the Iranian sociological/intellectual debates. Because when Iranian sociologists attempt to study historical issues related to America they do not know how to go to original sources or how to deconstruct mainstream narratives. Where can one find alternative approaches as far as America is concerned? The White-subjectivity has been the adjudicating norm in understanding the American society but Malcolm X represents a different subjectivity which could assist us in unlocking the riddles of the American Dream.

Why are restern social theorists unable in inventing creative modes of knowledge? In other words, why can't restern social theorists come up with novel forms of knowledge? Because they take up their leads from disciplinary forms of knowledge and read through Kant, Hegel, Marx, Durkheim, Small, Parsons, Weber, and Freud and so on and so forth. They think by reading through their texts they can become a social theorist but the truth of the matter is that these will not earn them any credibility as far as social theory is concerned. To put it differently, western social theorists did not turn into world-class sociologists by reading sociological texts. On the contrary, they invented forms of disciplinary knowledge by being immersed in various authentic traditions which have had longstanding backgrounds. In other words, in order to be able to become world-class social theorist the restern sociologists are in dire need of grasping the pre-sociological mode of envisioning which could assist us in inventing novel modes of knowledge. To do that we need to look at literature, poetry, jurisprudence, art, esoteric treatises, religious sermons, movies, folkloric tales and sagas and so on and so forth. Through immersing into these non-disciplinary forms of lore and knowledge then we may be able to come up with novel theories which are worth to be rated as world-class theories.

Very simply we could state that the problem with current literature on Malcolm X is that some just take a moralistic approach and argue that what made Malik El-Shabazz so great was that he bettered himself by acknowledging his mistakes, learning from them, and was committed to teaching the lessons of his mistakes to others, so others could better themselves. There are other approaches which could be summarized as "Blackening Discourse" and by that

I mean the proponents of this construction attempt to create a type of Malcolm X that is totally of "Black Essence." These blackening discourses seem interesting as they demonstrate some sort of critical approaches of sociological significance but they lack to demonstrate the global significance of Malcolm X's social theory. In other words, in despite of their intellectual rigor they are parochial in nature. Still there are some who attempt to disregard the historical contingencies in Malcolm X's biography by focusing only on "Islamic" period in a narrow sectarian fashion. Certainly one can find elements of each of these readings in Malcolm X's life and work and even one can surely discern other aspects and tendencies such as socialism, nationalism, Pan-Africanism, and Communism but these are not what have interested me in reading him. For me, he presents a social theorist with critical orientations which could assist us in creating novel approaches. What we need is a different reading of Malcolm X that is not of House-Negro Style but Field-Negro Style. However the difficult task is how to achieve such a different interpretative strategy which would enable us to see the theorist in Malcolm X? For unusual project one needs to travel on unusual paths as strangeness is the prime quality of modernity. In other words, modernity by definition is strange and to understand the contingent strangeness of *present human condition* one needs to capture strangeness through extra-ordinary fashions. Adrian Hill was a British artist and educator who coined the term *art therapy* in 1942. Hill thought that when the patient's physical resistance was at its lowest this somehow rendered the *animal ego* quiescent and allowed the creative powers of the *spiritual essence* to come through in works of art. He recognized that *conflict* was not only physically destructive but also damaged *minds*, *bodies* and *hopes*. In his interesting work *How To Draw* (1963) Hill talks about the role of "imagination" in developing on novel territories. Here I am not interested in drawing as such but I think in the present conflict-ridden world which humanity finds itself today we need to imagine outside established scholarly frames as adventure of this kind may "promise a sequence of unusual happenings" (Hill, 1963. 158). In other words, we need to conceptualize the legacy of Malcolm X through "drawing from imagination" (Hill, 1963. 158) as the traditional or accepted strategies "can only [produce] . . . illustrated make-believe" forms of knowledge which cannot deliver us from lope-sided vision of reality (Hill, 1963. 158).

Chapter One

Novel Strategies of Interpretation

NOVEL READING STRATEGIES

This is not a secret that Malcolm X has not been appropriated within the body of academic social sciences as he should have been. There are certainly institutional, epistemological, disciplinary, religious, ethnical, racial and ideological obstacles which could explain the underlying reasons for systematic negligence of Malcolm X in the mainstream debates on social theory. Having said this, it should be reemphasized that in the Iranian sociological context which defines itself in accordance to the logic of core and periphery the problems increase and by that I mean the absence of Malcolm X could not be solely explained by referring to indices such as institution, epistemology, discipline, religion, ethnicity, race or ideology. On the contrary, one needs to take into consideration other mechanisms which are less debated in the "core paradigm" such as inferiority complex, assimilation, alienation, westoxification, anti-state stance, and irrelevance.[1] In other words, social theorists who attempt to work without eurocentric parameters of sociology should realize that it is impossible to develop alternative/undisciplinary modes of theorizations without having *novel strategies of interpretation*. By novel strategies of interpretation, I refer to an approach which is based on minimizing the maximum and maximizing the minimum. In other words, within mainstream sociological contexts there are issues which are highlighted for certain reasons and there are questions which are relegated to the oblivion for systemic reasons. These strategies have created over consecutive years modes of understanding which function as "underlying assumptions" in any knowledge system and social theory is no exception in this regard. To put it differently, Malcolm X has been neglected for epistemic reasons which are justified within the knowledge system and this has contributed in *strategies of disengagement* as far as Malcolm X is concerned. Rules of engagement has produced strategies of disengagement and anybody who is interested in transcending boundaries of epistemic disengagement then the way out is not reproduction of engagement strategies. Said differently, one should recreate novel *reading strategies* which have been systematically suppressed in mainstream contexts of social theory. The first question which could enable us to develop different engaging strategies is whether one could consider Malcolm X as a social theorist as little is available on him in this regard. Reiland Rabaka argues that

> What is little known and/or rarely related is that Malcolm X's lifework and philosophical legacy register more than mere reaction to racism. Quite the contrary, Malcolm's social and political philosophy provides radical theorists with a new paradigm and point of departure for developing . . . critical theory of contemporary society (Rabaka, 2002. 145).

Rabaka is interested in reducing Malcolm X's legacy into African critical theory but I think his legacy is relevant for alternative social theorists who attempt to go beyond current modes of being which have been imposed upon diverse societies by capitalism. In other words, Malcolm X could assist us in breaking the rules of Epistemic Apartheid .

UNIFORM STRATEGIES OF READING

In order to understand the significance of Malcolm X we need to consult his approach to social problems which are profoundly of prophetic importance. Although he employs racial concepts in explaining his critical theory but it would be a mistake to read these concepts in uncreative fashions which would deprive us from implicit insights that are embedded in his outlook. One of the salient characteristics of creative social theorists is their ability to construct concepts based on local experiences which could have global or possibly universal implications. Of course, there are profound differences between global significance and universal importance but one could see degrees of universality in certain theoretical concepts which could be useful in theoretical generalizations within contexts of social theory. Malcolm X could be counted as one of undisciplinary social thinkers who have achieved certain level of theoretical complexities by constructing relevant local sociological concepts with global/universal consequences. In order to understand his sociological relevance we need to look at his two concepts of House Negro and Field Negro which are not even mentioned in the footnotes of Giddens' sociological textbook that are taught to students around the globe—even in Iran which purportedly has an anti-western policy in her higher education.

HOUSE NEGRO AND FIELD NEGRO

Malcolm X uses two concepts of House Negro and Field Negro in his theoretical endeavors. To understand this, he goes back to the story of slavery in America. He argues that there were

> Two kinds of slaves, the house Negro and the field Negro. The house Negroes—they lived in the house with master, they dressed pretty good, and they ate good because they ate his food—what he left. They lived in the attic or the basement, but still they lived near the master; and they loved the master more

than the master loved himself. They would give their life to save the master's house—quicker than the master would. If the master said, "We got a good house here," the house Negro would say, "Yeah, we got a good house here." Whenever the master said "we," he said "we." That's how you can tell a house Negro. If the master's house caught on fire, the house Negro would fight harder to put the blaze out than the master would. If the master got sick, the house Negro would say, "What's the matter, boss, we sick!" He identified himself with his master, more than his master identified with himself. And if you came to the house Negro and said, "Let's run away, let's escape, let's separate," the house Negro would look at you and say, "Man, you crazy. What you mean, separate? Where is there a better house than this? Where can I wear better clothes than this? Where can I eat better food than this?" That was that house Negro (1966. 10–11).

The questions of alienation and assimilation have been debated by social theorists in various fashions and here we can see that Malcolm X has his own approach to alienating and assimilating process of Black people in America. In his view, an alienated person is someone who has lost his/her own sense of subjectivity and incessantly attempts to identify him/herself with the master. Here we can deconstruct the terms which Malcolm employs in local frame of reference by reinterpreting key concepts which could be used in a more global or even universal sense. For instance, the concept of "master" could be reconfigured as "master-narrative" or "dominating mode of being" which in contemporary era could refer to eurocentric worldview or westernized model of social organization; the concept of "negro" could also be reinterpreted as "submissive mentalité" or "assimilated identity type." I would like even to argue that we can use the conceptual model provided by Malcolm X in relation to intellectual orientations which exist in restern world. For example, there are great many intellectuals, thinkers, writers, social theorists and philosophers in countries such as Iran, Turkey, Malaysia, Egypt, Pakistan, India, South Africa, Russia, Bosnia, Iraq,

Lebanon, Morocco, Tunisia, China, and so on and so forth who do not share the principles of eurocentric vision of reality. However this negation has come to be interpreted in terms of refusal of modernity as such and hence labeled as "enemies of modernity" or "anti-moderns." But the question is whether intellectuals such as Ali Shariati, Allama Iqbal, Taleghani, Bazargan, Seyyed M. B. Sadr, Seyyed M. Sadr, Said Nursi, Allama Tabatabai, Allama Jafari, Dostoevsky, Tolstoy, Jalal Al-e Ahmad, S. H. Alatas, S. M. N. Alatas and Sayyid Qtub are against modernity or their readings of modernity fall outside the parameters of eurocentric vision of modernity. This is to argue that whether we can talk about multiple modernities or there is a single linear type of modernity which should be applied universally all over the world without taking into consideration historical individualities. In addition to these questions we need to ponder upon scholarly models of interpretations which are dominant in academia that aspire to force upon "different texts"*uniform strategies of reading*. To highlight this, I can give an example which could clarify in details what I have in mind. John L. Esposito is one of the leading paradigm-makers of thinkers in the Muslim World. In his reading of makers of contemporary Islam he provides a dualistic vision whereby thinkers in the Islamic world are either seculars or religious and if they are the latter then surely they are operating within tradition versus modernity divide. This mode of reading texts within restern world is not only confined to John L. Esposito but it is a salient strategy of interpretation which is imposed by academic scholarship on restern intellectuals. Of course, I am certain that these strategies are beneficial and informative for certain political purposes but they are not faithful to texts and latent interplay which might exist in any intellectual text. First of all, these seemingly diverse thinkers are not homeless but belong to specific school of thought which I have termed as *primordial school of social theory*. Secondly the body of knowledge which has been produced by these scholars should not be interpreted solely within parameters of differences between modernity and tradition. On the contrary, I argue that by turning into texts which have been produced by these thinkers we can see that it is possible to have other forms of reading or different strategies of interpretation. These two notes lead us to the third issue which is related to Malcolm X and his interpretative strategy of deciphering as well as transcending alienating forms of being. In other words, the body of knowledge which is created by aforementioned thinkers and intellectuals could be conceptualized as alternative mode of being which is in contrast to submissive mentalité or "house negro" in the parlance of Malcolm X. To put it differently, I think to follow scholarly strategies of thinkers such as Esposito would not lead to any engaging understanding of primordial thinkers and the only possible outcome would be that they have attempted to reconcile tradition with modernity. But this is not how we should read them as there are plenty of evidences that they were aspiring to emancipate submissive mentality of restern people by creating alternative forms of subjectivities. This is to argue that they were attempting to draw the contours of "house subjectivity" by rebuking the foundations of "house intellectuality." In other words, to paraphrase the terminology of Malcolm X, one could argue that we should classify primordial thinkers as pioneers of "field intellectuals" rather than repeating the jargons of "house intellectuals" clad in religious terms. To put it differently, I think the concepts of house negro and field negro which have been coined by Malcolm X could assist us to redraw the map of intellectual activities beyond the parameters of eurocentric intellectual and scholarly paradigms. If Malcolm X is read in this fashion then his place within social theory should be reconsidered as these concepts along with other insights which he has left for us in terms of letters, epistles, speeches and articles could constitute the backbones of the Malcolmian Critical Social Theory.

ACADEMIC FORM OF ANALYSIS

When one speaks about sociological significance of Malcolm X some argue that he has not written any scholarly work a la Talcott Parsons or Emile Durkheim. This mode of understanding social theory is a very narrow-minded as there has been many other social theorists who never wrote the so-called scientific treaties. For instance, the importance of Antonio Gramsci could not be denied by any serious social theorist. But it is interesting to note that Gramsci has never been an academic sociologist in the institutional sense of the term and what he left behind bears no similarity to the scholarly articles of established sociologists who publish in prestigious journals in the world. On the contrary, the *Prison Notebooks* (*Quaderni del carcere*) were a series of notebooks written by Antonio Gramsci while he was imprisoned by the Italian Fascist regime in 1926. Although written unsystematically, the *Prison Notebooks* are considered a extremely innovative contribution to 20th century social theory and sociological vision of reality. Gramsci got inspirations from different sources—not only other Marxists but also theorists such as Niccolò Machiavelli, Vilfredo Pareto, Georges Sorel and Benedetto Croce. His notebooks include a wide range of topics, including history and the question of Italian nationalism, the question of the Enlightenment and its political manifestations, the Italian dictatorship, civil society, myths, religion and different phases of culture. The concept of cultural hegemony is associated with Gramsci and nobody can deny his importance in contemporary social theory even he did not have an "academic form of analysis" which is held as a criteria to ban thinkers and intellectuals to the pantheon of social theory. By a cursory look at the notes and speeches of Malcolm X we can find out that he is a type of social theorist which resembles Gramsci rather than Randall Collins but we should not confine the parameters of social theory to eurocentric patterns or strictly disciplinary modes of appropriation. If one could credit Gramsci for his contribution to social theory based on his definition of cultural hegemony, I think it is possible to consider Malcolm X as a highly original social theorist due to his concepts of house negro and field negro which could revolutionize our understanding of restern intellectual traditions outside the parameters of binary oppositions of modernity versus tradition.

The first question which could come to mind is that how could terms to be employed in a conceptual fashion and how concepts could be used in conceptualized fashion within parameters of sociological theory? Of course, these may seem very trivial questions by some critics but these are fundamental issues which have been taken for granted by professionally-oriented scholars who are indoctrinated in disciplinary modes of theorizing realities, human realities and social facts. In other words, if a thinker does not express his ideas within disciplinary forms of expressions then his body of ideas may not be received by disciplinary scholars who reside in institutions of social sciences. This is to argue that undisciplinary ideas shall remain as *terms* rather than *concepts*. Du Bois, for instance, was not considered as a sociologist due to the fact that his core ideas were centered around "race" rather than "rationality" or "capital" which determined the professional identity of sociology as a discipline in the beginning of the 20th century. But the transformations of world society forced the disciplinary architects of social sciences to revise their epistemological foundations by incorporating racial issues as core questions of social theory. By changing of strategy then the entire body of knowledge of Du Bois was incorporated into sociology and he was crowned as a sociologist. This makes us to reflect over the nature of sociological problems and how theories are made. In other words, are sociologists who make theories in their minds or social changes which bring about necessary materials of theories? If we agree that social changes and political transformations forced the discipline of sociology to reconsider the boundaries of disciplinarity then it is not very hard to argue that current changes in the world society shall force the discipline of sociology to reconsider the boundaries of *sociologicality*, disciplinarity and the significance of Malcolm X as a critical social theorist in the 21st century. The second question which could be raised in this context is that how could we conceptualize the key concepts of Malcolm X within parameters of social theory? In other words, in what fashion could we spot key terms within his body of ideas and transform them into conceptual tools which could be instrumental in sociological terms? To answer this question, I think we need to have a detour as the answer is not as simple as it may appear. We are accustomed to believe that problems are conceptualized due to their cognitive significance and based on epistemological relevance, sociologists work on social issues. But I think this is not a complete picture of how things function within the labyrinths of knowledge industry. In other words, it seems prior to this cognitive dimension there is an emotional aspect which precedes the "cognitive step." This is to argue that sociologist qua a human person is conditioned by emotive dimension before enters the realm of discipline which is a "cognitive form of engagement." Sociology as a discipline was born in the context of eurocentric vision of reality and this vision has colored the parameters of sociologists who have internalized uncritically the emotive vigor of eurocentrism. How could one break away from this iron cage which has conditioned the very parameters of modern identity qua a human being? Hybrid personalities who have lived in borderlands and at the crossroad of various traditions are equipped to carry on such a task. Of course, this is an important question which should be pondered upon by social theorists and philosophers who are interested in the sociology of human destiny in truly ontological sense of this concept.

NOTE

1. By anti-state stance, I refer to the positions of intellectuals, sociologists, thinkers, writers and social theorists who are very careful that their positions will

not look alike to the official position of the Islamist state in Iran. In other words, if the agenda of the state is to uphold global Islamist discourses then Iranian discourse-makers attempt to distance from any discourse which may bear similarity to the state ideology.

Chapter Two

Undisciplinary Fields of Knowledge

DESCARTES VERSUS RUMI

I divide world-class theorists within the context of social theory into two broad categories of "heart theorists" and "mind theorists." Although I have never seen anybody to classify social theorists into heart versus mind but I find this distinction a very useful analytical category which enables me to step beyond the disciplinary categories which, by definition, is Cartesian, i.e. *cognitive* rather than Rumian, i.e. *cordetive*. If this distinction is of any relevance then I like to argue that Malcolm X is more of a cordetive theorist rather than cognitive which is deeply indebted to the Cartesian mentalité which imbues the total frame of disciplinary reference. Although one may argue that there is no textual reference in the works and letters of Malcolm X to Rumi then how could one argue that he has incorporated the Rumian perspective in his social outlook? First of all, when it is argued that Malcolm X is not a Cartesian theorist it does not mean that he does not employ cognitive categories in his frame of analysis. Secondly if one argues that Malcolm X is a Rumian social theorist this does not mean that he has employed Rumi's ideas in his social analyses as what is meant by being a Rumian social theorist is an attempt to distinguish the overall orientation of Malcolm X rather than arguing that he did not use rational categories in his approach. These are different arguments. Thirdly, what it is meant by the cognitive orientation versus the cordetive approach is an onto-epistemic question which alerts us to see the differences between fields of knowledge in undisciplinary fashions. In other words, this analytical distinction would permit us to see forms of knowledge beyond the parameters of disciplinary forms of epistemes. Of course, this is not to argue in a reified fashion that certain social theorists think solely by their mind without realizing that they have other forms of acquiring knowledge but this argument is surely based on the assumption that some social theorists prefer to exclude the epistemological importance of cordetive dimensions. This is an epistemological conflict which has ontic root and I think the Cartesian mode of understanding represents the *cognitive form of perception* while the Rumian model of comprehension demonstrates the *cordetive modality of engaging* with reality. Why is this distinction important within social sciences discourses? In other words, what is the benefit of arguing that Malcolm X is a Rumian social theorist and not a Cartesian social scientist? What are the consequences of such an analytical distinction? I think both of these models and forms are informative and formative for human societies but the difference I guess it lies in the fine line which may exists between different kinds of beneficiaries. In other words, who is the prime beneficiary of social knowledge? Is the human individual or state actors or corporate agents? In my view, cordetive modality of engagement is a form of knowledge that benefits individual citizenry while the cognitive form of knowledge is useful for different forms of controlling social regimes-which are best represented by state apparatuses or corporate companies nowadays. Malcolm X represents the cordetive form of knowledge which equips oppressed individuals who have been under panoptican spell of stupification (in Shariatian sense) and desperately look for liberation. But liberation cannot come about if we put collective liberation before the individual self-realization and personal self-consciousness. The disciplinary mode of knowledge seems to focus on grand entities such as "History," "Nation," "State," "Civilization," "Humanity," "Culture," "Society," and "God" and so on and so forth. These concepts are useful analytically but when they are perceived as realities then we are lost as we think when society is progressing this should automatically mean that we, as individuals, are becoming better people in comparison to our predecessors. Dostoevsky argues about the paradoxes of disciplinary mode of engaging with reality in his Brothers Karamazov, where he talks about the mother of Liza in the presence of Father Zosima. She confides before Father Zosima that she loves humanity but she cannot tolerate people who live around her. In other words, her love for humanity as a grand concept is limitless but when it comes to her neighbour she has zero tolerance. To put it in Dostoevsky's own words, where he argues through the mother of Liza's character by arguing that

> I, generally, love humanity but I am surprised by my own stance as when I look carefully . . . I realize that more I love humanity in general less I feel sympathy towards individual human beings. In my dreams, I always see myself as a philanthropist who is incessantly ready to be at the service of humanity but I find myself unable to share a room with someone during daytime even for a short while. By experience I have come to realize that whenever someone approaches me I feel he has injured my sense of dignity and violated my sense of freedom. It is not hard to imagine that I may lose interest and grow feelings of hatred and enmity toward the world's most perfect man . . . after a day of being at his presence . . . I may hate someone for having his lunch slowly . . . or another one due to his running nose . . . or as soon as someone touches me I feel hatred toward all people. However what I want to say is that more I love humanity as a general idea but my feelings toward individual human beings are full of revulsion and resentment (Dostoevsky, 2009. 72).

Why is she like that? What was Dostoevsky trying to say by using these different characters? I think he was implicitly making distinction between the Cartesian mode of engaging with reality and the Rumian model of mentalité which are expressed as cognitive approach versus cordetive approach.

TUTELAGE AND THE RIDDLE OF SUBJECTIVITY

How does a personality come to reality? In other words, what are the constitutive elements of personal realization? There are many studies on identity-building in human sciences discourses but if we could generalize the nub of these important researches one may be able to summarize it with one broad concept of "subjectivity." But what is subjectivity? Is it a contradictory concept which stands in contrast to "objectivity" or a complimentary concept to the latter? Subjectivity is the condition of being a subject: i.e., the quality of possessing perspectives, experiences, feelings, beliefs, desires, and/ or power. Authors such as Dallmayr (1981), Farrell & Farrell (1994), Lauer (1958), Ellis (1992) and Bowie (1990) conceptualize subjectivity as a repertoire which is used as an explanation for what influences and informs people's judgments about truth or reality. In this line of reading it is the collection of the perceptions, experiences, expectations, personal or cultural understanding, and beliefs specific to a person. However what makes this line of interpretation peculiar is the fact that it is often used in contrast to the term objectivity, which is described as a view of truth or reality which is free of any individual's influence. Although we agree that subjectivity belongs to a person's particular vision of reality based on various contingent aspects but this concept is not in contrast to objectivity if by that contradistinction one attempts to have a subjectivistic interpretation of subjectivity. On the contrary, when we use the concept of "subjectivity" in this context we refer to the importance of individual assessment of objective conditions which one may find oneself in. In this line of reading there is no insistence upon binary opposition or superiority of one over against the other. In addition, subjectivity could be better understood when its lack is observed, i.e. when one is unable to have an interpretation of reality based on her/his own perception and instead relies on others' vision of reality. Here a sense of tutelage may emerge which could have grave sociopolitical consequences when the destiny of a group of people is at stake. To put it differently, when in social conditions where there are various contrasting interests and conflicts involved if a particular group gets the upper hand by consolidating its own perceptions of reality as the criteria of reality as such then seeds of oppressions and suppressions may emerge. This could be formulated in other fashions too namely if the subjectivity of a particular group becomes equal to objectivity of all groups and this is what Shariati conceptualizes as stupification, i.e. the lack of authentic subjectivity. Of course, one may ask how this could occur. In other words, how could alienation be perceived as actualization without using brute force? In my reading of Malcolm X I have come to realize that he is one of the contemporary primordial social theorists who have paid consistent attention to the question of individual alienation and collective estrangement. Of course, he has used particular terms such as "Black," and "Negro" and his focus has been on specific contexts such as America and Afro-Americans but one could deconstruct these specific terms and reconstruct them in global as well as universal frames of references. Malcolm X talks about two kinds of mentalities or forms of subjectivities. The first one is house-negro subjectivity which is based on the other's subjectivity and surprisingly is construed as objectivity. In other words, the house-negro understands deep affection but projects his love toward his master. The master who happens to be a white is the core of house-negro's reality. The house-negro associates his sense of selfhood with the other or what Malcolm terms as "master." Malcolm uses a figurative language by arguing that the house-negro would renounce all he has at his disposal just for the simple reason of being close to the master. In other words, the house-negro does not have any sense of being in an authentic sense and there is nothing that he would like to associate himself by except the subjective sense of the master which is the only objective reality that he can perceive as a twisted human personality. Malcolm explains this twisted sense of being in the following fashion, i.e.

> House Negro loves his master. He wants to live near him. He'll pay three times as much as the house is worth just to live near his master, and then brag about I'm the only Negro out here. I'm the only one on my job. I'm the only one in this school." You're nothing but a house Negro. And if someone comes to you right now and says, Let's separate, you say the same thing that the house Negro said on the plantation. What you mean, separate? From America, this good white man? Where you going to get a better job than you get here? I mean, this is what you say. I ain't left nothing in Africa, that's what you say. Why you left your mind in Africa" (1966. 11).

Malcolm X knew that you cannot unshackle an imprisoned folk who is not only physically enchained but mentally enslaved without waking them up to a different kind of consciousness. In other words, slavery annihilated the sense of being a subject in the hearts of Afro-Americans and the only thing which could change the status quo was revolution. But what kind of revolution could bring such a drastic sense of transformation in the hearts and minds of enslaved people who could not even realize that they have lost their sense of humanity? In the eyes of Malcolm X what could qualify an individual as a human person it is his sense of subjectivity but once you lose that and you do not even realize that you have lost your own humanity then no political revolution could occur. Because the house-negro mentality is tantamount to stupification which entails a *total loss of subjectivity* and in Malcolm X's perspective it was conceptualized as a sense of assimilation which is symbolized by the concept of America. In other words, Malcolm X uses two concepts of America and Africa as symbols of stupification and emancipation.

SYMBOLISM UNTHOUGHT

Many have tried to understand the concepts of *America* and *Africa* in concrete sense but the symbolical dimensions of Malcolm X's interpretations have been lost for various reasons and one of the most important reasons is that scholars on X are not clear about how one should read the legacy of Malcolm X. In order to understand the lack of proper reading strategies vis-à-vis Malcolm X we need to look at three factors; the first one is the dominance of the Whites in America which created a sense that Malcolm should only be understood in White terms but in a *reversed fashion*; the second question is the presence of *total racism* which gave a false sense that the sole mission of Malcolm X was to combat racism by all means necessary; the third issue is related to hegemonic dominance of the Cold War discourses which could not even imagine the birth of alternative discourses outside the parameters of left or right. To put it differently, we have few scholars who are able to read the legacy of Malcolm X in alternative fashions namely in terms of symbolic interpretation. I can give an example by reference to one of the passages where Malcolm X talks about America, Africa, Separation, Mind, and Exodus. In his speech entitled as *Message to the Grassroots* he talks about "separation" between the whites and blacks in America and even proposes that the black community should get back to Africa. In addition, he construes the arguments of his opponents who refute this idea as a foolish strategy by arguing that Afro-Americans have not left anything in Africa. In other words, the opponents of Malcolm X were surprised that he had still an African mentalité. Malcolm X puts these issues in the following passage by stating that

> If someone comes to you right now and says, Let's separate, you say . . . What you mean, separate? From America, this good white man? Where you going to get a better job than you get here? I mean, this is what you say. I ain't left nothing in Africa, that's what you say. Why you left your mind in Africa (1966. 11).

American scholars both white and black due to their closeness to the issues which Malcolm X was addressing and discussing about took everything literally and this made impossible for them to discern symbolical nuances in Malcolm X's thought. In addition, due to the fact that Malcolm X's *frage* turned into a national security question then any research on him was deeply clouded by a vulgar reading of this visionary thinker of 21st century. To put it otherwise, Malcolm X was talking about different symbols and each of these symbols represented something for him; i.e. America represented *tutelage*; Africa stood for *emancipation*; Separation referred to the possibility of a kind of dialectic, i.e. alienation from the master and actualization into new modes of being; and the African mind was a symbol of *authentic subjectivity*.

Many scholars who have worked upon Malcolm X seem to disregard these novel dimensions in his intellectual legacy due to the *a priori* perspectives which they hold even before entering the intellectual world of Malcolm X. What we need to do as field intellectuals is that we have to de-white him, de-black him; de-left him and instead establish new strategies of readings which could enable us to *unthink* the legacy of Malcolm X.

FIELD[1] STRATEGIES OF RESISTANCE

We have argued that a human personality needs to be built upon an authentic sense of subjectivity which, in turn, is founded upon experiences, feelings, beliefs, and desires among many other pivotal issues. One of the salient characteristics of human being is her/his ability to love and hate. But the question is what is love or hate? There are many different definitions of these terms within social sciences and humanities discourses but here we are interested in this question in regard to Malcolm X's perspective on field-negro mentalité which is a form of self-actualized personality that Malcolm X developed to explain strategies of resistance before the hegemonic power of the *other*—which reduces you to an objectified nothing. In this context, we are interested in Malcolm X's approach to "hatred" as it seems the concept of field-negro is construed in a dialectical mode which is based upon hatred as a sense of keeping away one's suppressed self from the destructive treatment of the other. James W. Underhill, in his *Ethnolinguistics and Cultural Concepts: truth, love, hate & war*, (2012) conceptualizes diverse modalities of hate in different linguistic contexts. He emphasizes that love and hate are constructions of social and cultural origins. Therefore, revulsion is contextualized within complex patterns of historicities. Even though it is reasonable to argue that one single emotion exists in English, French (haine), and German (Hass), hate varies in the forms in which it is expressed. A certain relationless hatred is expressed in the French expression *J'ai la haine*, which has no equivalent in English. While for English-speakers, loving and hating invariably involve an object, or a person, and therefore, a relationship with something or someone, *J'ai la haine* (literally, I have hate) precludes the idea of an emotion directed at a person. This is a form of frustration, apathy and animosity which churns within the subject but establishes no relationship with the world, other than an aimless desire for destruction. Based on Underhill's approach one could argue that Malcolm X's forms of anti-Americanism is a specific form of cultural resentment (Underhill, 2012). In other words, the kind of hatred which Malcolm X talks about is a relational hate which is directed at a group that has imposed certain forms of oppressive regimes upon, in this Malcolmian context, the Black Community in America. Malcolm

X uses the concept of "hatred" in a psychoanalytic fashion, i.e. as an ego state that wishes to destroy the source of its unhappiness (Freud, 1915). Malcolm X did not consider the source of unhappiness of the Afro-Americans in the United States of America as a matter of rationalization or capitalism but he thought the source of misery is systematic racism which imbues the system in all its dimensions. When you are in such an inhumane context then you look surely for ways to liberate yourself and this is the question which lied before Malcolm X as a visionary social thinker. His explicit answers may be of parochial importance but the implicit dimensions of his discourse are important too as they could be employed for building up alternative modes of knowledge. In other words, he attempted to create a sense of unease in the minds of black people in America who seemed to be happy with their stupefied state of social life due to what Malcolm termed as the house-negro mentality, i.e. the state of being benumbed or unable to use their faculties in full capacities. But the question is how to create such a form of awareness within the hearts of people who are so deeply benumbed that they cannot realize the true reasons of their cultural tutelage? Malcolm X uses history as a means to bring forms of awareness to the minds of people who have lost touch with their own facticities. Sometimes he argues that one of the main problems with assimilated people is that they think they are one with their masters and in so thinking they lose their authentic sense of identity. He argues that during the slavery era we had two kinds of identities among slaves, i.e. the house Negro and the field Negro. Then Malcolm goes on explaining the features of the Field Negro. He argues that on

> That same plantation, there was the field Negro. The field Negroes—those were the masses. There were always more Negroes in the field than there were Negroes in the house. The Negro in the field caught hell. He ate leftovers. In the house they ate high up on the hog. The Negro in the field didn't get any-

thing but what was left of the insides of the hog. They call it chitt'lings nowadays. In those days they called them what they were—guts. That's what you were—gut-eaters. And some of you are still gut-eaters. The field Negro was beaten from morning to night: he lived in a shack, in a hut; he wore old, castoff clothes. He hated his master. He was intelligent. That house Negro loved his master, but that . . . field Negro . . . remember, they were in the majority, and they hated the master. When the house caught on fire, he didn't try to put it out; that field Negro prayed for a wind, for a breeze. When the master got sick, the field Negro prayed that he'd die. If someone came to the field Negro and said, Let's separate, let's run, he didn't say Where we going? He'd say, Any place is better than here. I am a field Negro. The masses are the field Negroes (1966. 11).

In other words, the house Negro was trapped in a false sense of consciousness and therefore he loved his master, i.e. he was happy with his own state of wretchedness. On the other hand, Malcolm presents another form of Negro who is able to distinguish between the state of tutelage and the state of enlightenment and that is what he conceptualizes as the Field Negro. But this kind of social type could not emerge if one is unable to demarcate between one's true sense of being and one's enslaved state of being in society. Malcolm X argues that the field-negro-mentalité is based on indignation because the field Negro "hated his master" (X, 1966. 11), i.e. he was aware that what the social source of his unhappiness was and wished to "destroy the source of [his] unhappiness" (Freud, 1915. 111). But it is wrong to assume that Malcolm X's social philosophy is based on hatred as hate is a strategy to raise consciousness among a benumbed group of people who are not aware of their state of tutelage. In other words, we should distinguish between strategy and vision of Malcolm X as far as fundamentals of his social theory is concerned. To put it differently, the politics of Malcolm X employs abhorrence to destroy political obstacles which exists on the way of erecting an egalitarian society but the critical theory of Malcolm X is not based on hatred. This is a fine issue which seems to be missed in Anglo-American literature on Malcolm X as a social theorist.

NOTE

1. It should be realized that the concept of "Field" in this study is employed in the Malcolmian sense which is epitomized in the two concepts of House Negro versus Field Negro. In other words, the concept of "Field" in the Malcolmian paradigm means emancipation, self-actualization, biophilic rather than necrophilic.

Chapter Three

Violence, Religion, and Extremism

MILITANT SECULARISM AND FANATIC RELIGIONISM

It is not a secret that the world is in a mess. The scope of chaos is not regional but global in nature and like a virus moves all over the world with an unprecedented speed. Many scholars and distinguished intellectuals across the globe have attempted to address questions which are directly or indirectly related to violence, extremism and mass suicides either under the banner of religion or the so-called humanitarian-bombing-paradigm/humanitarian-peace-bombing-paradigm. Regardless of posteriori reasons which are made up by politicians and terrorists for their inhumane activities the results are surprisingly similar in both camps, i.e. devastating forms of atrocities around the globe. But the question is how should we understand the current situation? The roots of these atrocities lie in *militant secularism* and *fanatic religionism*. Both of these perspectives are totalitarian in nature and do not allow any free space for the *truly different*. The militant secularism bans all forms of beings under the pretext of "transcultural reason" and the fanatic religionism forbids all forms of knowledge by resorting to a "mythical pure perception." In both of these readings the living forms are negated any kind of relevance and doomed to be re-formed along the abstract form of reason and mythical mode of perception. In other words, the problems which have overwhelmed humanity today are not only of political nature but they have intellectual roots which should be attended if we are serious about tackling them. If we focus on the political dimension alone then we shall repeat the stupidities of our forefathers but in different forms and modalities which could have destructive consequences beyond sound imagination. In this context, we think the outlook of Malcolm X is of great significance as he realizes the important dynamism of religion in the public square, on the one hand, but he, at the same time, does not disregard the significance of diversity in matters of society, politics and culture. In his speech in the Cleveland on April 3, 1964, he makes clear that he is a Muslim but the problem is that this concept is not an innocent term today. We see images of people who shout on top of their voices that they are Muslims but commit abhorrent atrocities against fellow Muslims or fellow human beings on different channels on TV every now and then. In other words, we need to have a critical approach toward the concept of "Muslim" and see in what sense Malcolm employed this term as this is a controversial issue in a post-globalized world. In his view, religion is not a means for oppression but a medium for inquiry and this distinction is of pivotal significance. He argues that "I'm still a Muslim . . . [but] . . . I'm not here to try and change your religion" (1966. 24). What does this mean? What does he mean by being a Muslim and not desiring to change the religious views of the others? In a *missionary mindset* of both militant secularism and fanatic religionism which embraces all dimensions of our life today, it is hard to understand what Malcolm X stands for. In other words, why should he argue that the dialog is possible even when we have differences? To be more accurate, it seems Malcolm X is of the opinion that dialog is only possible when we not only concede to the principle of diversity but also celebrate differences as the absence of diversity would benumb the possibility of growth in the world of humanity. To put it differently, he was convinced that diversity was not only a fact but also a "divine sign," i.e. a means for manifestation of divinity in the world of humanity—and as such it should be cherished and employed as a fertile form of dialog. If this is a sane argument then both forms of exclusivist interpretations of militant secularism and fanatic religionism should be combated as modes of politics and religiosity in the public square.

In other words, it is possible to envision Malcolm X's approach to human problems in a non-secular as well as non-religious fashion which celebrates diversity without denying one's own identity. However, there are scholars who have approached Malcolm X differently and argue that he was a militant and fanatic. Was he a militant and fanatic? In other words, it is impossible to employ the legacy of Malcolm X in overcoming militancy, extremism, violence and sectarianism in a divided world which we find ourselves today.

Some may argue that Malcolm X's position is ethnocentrism or "inverted racism," i.e. Black Racism against the racism waged on Afro-Americans by the Whites. Although it is undeniable that there is a rage in X's speeches but it is wrong to assume that he is a black racist or Muslim fanatics. Why do I argue this? Could this claim be backed up by solid evidence? Are there references in his work which could support my argument?

In his speech which was delivered in the Cleveland on April 3, 1964, Malcolm X talked on a serious political question which he entitled it "The Ballot or the Bullet." In this speech he argued that although

> I'm still a Muslim, I'm not here tonight to discuss my religion. I'm not here to try and change your religion. I'm not here to argue or discuss anything that we differ about, because it's time for us to submerge our differences and realize that it is best for us to first see that we have the same problem, a common problem. . . . Whether you are educated or illiterate, whether you live

on the boulevard or in the alley, you're going to catch hell just like I am. We're all in the same boat and we all are going to catch the same hell from the same man. He just happens to be a white man. All of us have suffered here, in this country, political oppression at the hands of the white man, economic exploitation at the hands of the white man, and social degradation at the hands of the white man. Now in speaking like this, it does not mean that we're anti-white, but it does mean we're anti-exploitation, we're anti-degradation, and we're anti-oppression. And if the white man doesn't want us to be anti-him, let him stop oppressing and exploiting and degrading us (1966. 24–5).

I quoted this in length to show the spirit and the content of Malcolm X where he makes a clear distinction between "biological racism"—which was elaborated by Ku Klux Klan, on the one hand, and early phases of the Nation of Islam at the hands of Elijah Muhammad, on the other hand—and "cultural racism"—which could have socio-politico-economic reasons and for such underlying reasons the proponents of exploitation support "apparent racial ideologies" for keeping others in submissive modes of life.

In other words, Malcolm X makes a distinction between "inherent racism of the White" and "accidental racism of the White" by arguing that the White Man "just happens to be" (1966.24) the political oppressor, economic exploiter, and social degrader of the Black Man "in this country" (1966.24). To put it differently, if we could change the oppressive system then Malcolm would argue that *"we're [not] ... anti-white ... but we're anti-exploitation, ... anti-degradation, ... anti-oppression"* (1966. 24–5).

This mode of analysis transforms the theoretical configuration of Malcolm X's social theory by making it transculturally relevant and humanistically significant due to the fact that he addresses the "real riddles" of the capitalist world-system which is based on "oppression," "exploitation," and "degradation" of the *other*—both within the state and outside the political boundaries of the state. Said differently, racism may be a fundamental element in race-conscious or race-plagued cultures but if there was not any race problem we should not rest in peace in a context which is based on "OED," i.e. oppression/exploitation/degradation. Because today we may not have racial problem as we had in the 20th century but "OED" is not over yet as the system could stay alive as long as it does not yield into ideals of justice, fraternity, equality and liberty. In other words, Malcolm X seems to argue that the world capitalist system is not the defender of the Enlightenment Ideals of Justice, Fraternity, Equality and Liberty. On the contrary, it is its destroyer *par excellence* due to the fact that it could only prolong its life as long as a world based on such ideals is not born. The ideals of Enlightenment are the anti-thesis of the capitalism which uses racism, as it did in the 20th century in USA, as an instrument for creating systematic hate, systemic violence, societal division, organized conflict, studied crises and planned war between nations and in the hearts of people so they could not care about each other or lest unite under the same flag of Fraternity, Justice, Liberty and Equality. Malcolm X, by moving away from "biological racism" freed himself from "inverted racism" and also made his discourse more of universal significance—which could be employed by alternative social theorists who are seeking to understand the underlying mechanisms of tutelage of the "restern world" before the "eurocentric global hegemony."

RACIAL REVOLUTION

By living in Euro-America one could realize that the Euro-Atlantic civilization is one of the most over-conscious and over-sensitive social structures as far as the race and color are concerned. However, it is interesting to note that most of the giants of disciplinary social theory such as Freud, Marx, Durkheim, Weber, Small, Parsons and Pareto do never talk about the racial structures of the modern society and how the racially-motivated elements could overshadow the potentials of social structures as well as contours of human agency. The story of sociology was founded upon *Western White Male* (WWM) and in this fashion the mentality of founding constructors of disciplinary social theory conceptualized the Black people in America as the *colored people*. In other words, the subconscious of Anglo-American subject was so deeply engaged with the issue of race that the demarcative lines between various people were constructed along the issue of "skin color." This racial attitude was not only confined to lay people but it included all strata of white society both in Europe and America. The founding fathers of sociologists did not fare any better in this regard as most of early social scientists preferred to employ the *dismissive strategy* even in discursive contexts. For instance, in modern American history a myth was constructed by mainstream social scientists that the Blacks were responsible for the failures of the *Reconstruction Era*. This orthodox view was not challenged by any of key white founding fathers of American social theorists such as Albion Small or Talcott Parsons. Although they were conceptualizing social theory in the so-called universal terms but issues of race and ethnicities which were haunting the American society escaped their attention in a complete fashion. But this pivotal question did not go unattended by one of the key sociologists, i.e. W. E. B. Du Bois who realized that the main issue of American social theory is not the question of rationality but race. In other words, Du Bois challenged the myth of universality concocted by disciplinary social scientists, on the one hand, and he, on the other hand, demonstrated that social theory could not be a theory of all societies but particular society. This is to argue that we cannot talk about social theory without taking into consideration burning issues of particular society. To put it differently, in a racially conscious society of America the dismissive strategy of Parsons on racial questions speaks about a malaise which needs to be conceptualized sociologically but this was not discussed until early years of 80s in the 20th century. But

Du Bois was years ahead than other White Western Male sociologists who disregarded the question of race in the constitution of self and society in the context of America. The question of the *Reconstruction Era* is one of the key questions which one can discern the partisan interpretations of White social theorists against the Black People in USA. In 1935, he published his *Black Reconstruction in America* and there he challenged the prevailing orthodoxy that blacks were responsible for the failures of the Reconstruction era (Du Bois, 1935). It seems that Du Bois believed that racism is an offshoot of capitalism and this conviction led him to choose Socialism as his ideological frame of analysis. In other words, it could be argued that Du Bois is more in line with Marxist theories of capitalism according to which colonialism and imperialism are high stages of capitalism. Racism, in this line of interpretation, provides the ideological justification for colonialism and imperialism. But what has Du Bois to do with Malcolm X? Why is Du Bois important in reimagining of Malcolm X? As I mentioned earlier there are few who have looked at Malcolm X in terms of sociological theory and social theory but even those few who have paid scant attention to his intellectual legacy seem to read him in a Du Boisian fashion. This is to argue that they attempt to interpret Malcolm X in a fashion that he will appear at the end as a Du Boisian critical theorist who views racism in a Marxist mode of analysis. By establishing this interpretative strategy, the American scholars have been able to read him in a Marxist fashion and also minimize the importance of Islamism or Political Islam in Malcolm X's frame of analysis. Although it is accepted that he has not developed very extensively on Islamism in his critical theory but there are ample references that he has not taken Islam solely as a *form of devotion* but a way of political strategy in rectifying the ills of society. For instance, in his speech entitled *The Ballot or the Bullet* he states that although *"I'm still a Muslim, I'm not here to discuss my religion but* [find a solution] *for a common problem* [which we suffer from] *in this country; political oppression at the hands of the white man"* (1966. 24). This is to argue that he interprets religion as a frame of political action and in so doing he comes very close to the position of advocates of Islamism within the parameters of liberation theology or social theology. In other words, his position on social issues is not of theological nature but sociological one and this would assist us to differentiate between his inclusive Islamist position and those of extremist Salafism of today, on the one hand, and highlight the fundamental differences between the socialist position of Du Bois and Islamist position of Malcolm X, on the other hand. These are issues which need to be discussed by anyone who is interested in the politics of social theory in the American context as well as in regard to the global context of Islamism and social theory.

Now let us go back to the question of race and its relation to the American society in Malcolm X's view which seems to differ from the position of Du Bois who was also critical of racial politics in USA but believed that racism is an offshoot of capitalism. There are certain passages in Malcolm X's works where one can find references to racism as a product of society rather than an inherent biological tendency. For instance, in Haryou-Act Forum, December 12, 1964, he explained his position to the American ambassador in Africa by arguing that

> I told him, "What you're telling me, whether you realize it or not, is that it is not basic in you to be a racist, but that society there in America, which you all have created, makes you a racist." This is true; this is the *worst* racist society on this earth. There is no country on earth which you can live and racism be brought out in you—whether you're white or black—more so than this country that poses as a democracy. This is a country where the social, economic, political atmosphere creates a sort of psychological atmosphere that makes it almost impossible, if you're in your right mind, to walk down the street with a *white* person and not be self-conscious, or he or she not be self-con-

scious. It almost can't be done, and it makes you *feel* this racist tendency that pops up. But it's the society itself (1966. 214).

Here we can see that racism is a complex result of various socio-politico-economic factors along with psychological features but there are other instances where Malcolm X seems to suggest a contradictory view on racism. For instance, by arguing that in the West,

> There has been much talk about a population explosion. Whenever [the Whites] are speaking of the population explosion, in my opinion they are referring primarily to the people in Asia or in Africa—the Black, Brown, Red, and Yellow people. It is seen by people of the West that, as soon as the standard of living is raised in Africa and Asia, automatically the people begin to reproduce abundantly. And there has been a great deal of fear engendered by this in the minds of the people of the West, who happen to be, on this earth, a very small minority. In fact, in most of the thinking and planning of Whites in the West today, it's easy to see the fear . . . [which] . . . governs their political views and . . . it governs their economic views and it governs most of their attitudes toward present society . . . the social structure [of the modern world system] . . . [is like a] . . . racial powder keg . . . [which lies beneath the capitalist social structures] (1966. 45–6).

In other words, it looks like Malcolm X oscillates between two different positions; in the first position he is suggesting that racism is a product of social organization while in the second position it seems he considers capitalist social organization as a product of racism. However, I think there may be a third possibility here too, namely I don't think he is claiming causality of capitalism. Rather, he is arguing that white racism causes underdevelopment of blacks. To put it differently, the question is about the relationship between white racism and capitalism. It seems he attaches a specific accent on the socio-cultural organization of the White culture within the parameters of capitalism which has no equal in other forms of racism. In other words, the black people cannot redeem and emancipate themselves from their oppressed position if they take the *Negrofragae* in Marxist or Du Boisian frame of references. Here it seems the question of religion plays a significant role as Christianity has played a pivotal role in domesticating the Black people by not only justifying slavery but enslaving their minds too. In other words, for the Black community (and all the oppressed nations around the globe) it is necessary to alienate themselves from the symbolic universe of the White and this strategy will enable them to actualize their authentic self anew. Seen in this fashion, then one could understand why Malcolm chose Islam as a religion for his struggle against racism in America and not Christianity. In addition, this could explain that in what sense he followed Du Bois and where he differed from the Du Boisian frame of envisioning the future of the Black People in America. In sum, it could be emphasized that Malcolm X sees a close link between the structures of America and the world capitalist social organization and at its heart he discerns the problem of "race" rather than "Das Kapital," "Rationality," or "Anomie." This is a question which is better understood and conceptualized in post-racial discourses than in mainstream/eurocentric paradigms of disciplinary social sciences.

HISTORIOGRAPHY OF REVOLT/REVOLUTION IN SOCIOLOGY

Turning-points are the keys for understanding the underlying frames of references in the constitution of self and society. It could be argued that a turning-point is a time at which a decisive change in a situation occurs, especially one with crucial results. Although it is a temporal event but it has spatial consequences and its corollaries would transform the ways through which one perceives reality as such. In other words, a turning-point is a type of perspectival *feng shui*, i.e. a conceptual system of arranging one's location in the configuration of things in the myriad forms of realities. To put it differently, as the feng shui practice discusses architecture in metaphoric terms of *invisible forces* that bind the universe, earth, and man together, a turning-point makes sense of unknown accidents which surround one at some point of time in a specific context. Said differently, by attaching a significant importance to a particular turning-point we prefer one interpretation of an event (or series of events) over against the other interpretations. In other words, talking about turning-points is always tantamount to choosing an interpretative system over its competing forms of analyses. This is to argue that a turning-point is not simply a historical event which has occurred and observable by everyone regardless of their points of departures. On the contrary, a turning-point is a point which is more of philosophical significance than merely a historical accident which has taken place in a particular place at a specific time. In other words, each society, each group, each epoch and each tradition may have their own particular turning-points which may not be upheld as significant by those who do not share the meaning-blocks of society A versus society B or tradition C versus tradition D. If one could distinguish between history and historiography then it would be readily accepted that "universal turning-points" are not easy to define as defining moments may differ in each context depending on one's vector. But why is it important to be wary about turning-points in humanities, social sciences and, in particular, in the context of social theory? In sum, a turning point could be defined as a fundamental change in one's perception of the past that occurs in a historical time and has a far-reaching influence in the later period. Such turning points should lead to the rise of new ruptures in history, hence contributing to a new form of living that (re)shapes one's vision of the past, the present, and the future. This new mode can exert its influence within its own culture, or without, having a global, cross-cultural impact. In other words, a turning point involves deeply the question of legitimacy in its most fundamental fashion, i.e. who has the final verdict upon defining the complex patterns of reality as a whole. For instance, the year 1968 plays a vital position in the context of disciplinary social theory for anybody who considers it as a turning-point. The future of humanity in a global sense is, for example, defined in terms of the 1968 revolt in France by Rojas who argues that the

> post-1968 Europe has ceased to be the radiating center of the dominating culture of the Western World, at the same time in which music, sculpture, painting and the arts of all the regions of the world become universal and are disseminated everywhere, asserting themselves as so many other cultural, alternative and possible cosmovisions have within the new situation of cultural and social polycentrism. These are movements where centers decline. And where the role itself of centrality as a global mechanism of social functioning is delegitimized in its own foundations, which may basically express the opening of a new and radically different situation of world capitalism, that after 1968–73 began entering into a clear situation of historical "bifurcation." This situation of divergence in which the mechanisms of stabilization and reproduction of the world capitalist system as a whole ceased to function, announcing its inevitable end as well as the pressing need for its deep mutation and transformation. Following Immanuel Wallerstein's incisive hypothesis, we could ask ourselves if 1968 did not then have, in addition to its profound character as a global reaching cultural revolution with civilizing consequences, a new and additional supplementary significance: that of having inaugurated with its irruption, this clearly terminal phase of the life of modern capitalism that was initiated more or less five centuries ago. However, as we have well been reminded by the "soixante-huitard" generation the world over, history is not an automatic process with is inevitably one way, but rather it is a process carried out by men themselves, who with our collective action and our reflections help to decide their possible destinies, in accordance with the

conditions of possibility of each specific historic moment (Rojas, 2004. 213-4).

Said differently, 1968 is considered as the symbolic sign by which every aspect of meaningfulness should be weighed by and this has become like a bizarre mantra where eurocentric sociologists conceptualize the history of modern world in terms which are deeply parochial rather than universal. This is to restate that1968 is one of those dates which have been conceptualized as a "turning-point" in the context of social theory. This cliché has been internalized by the Iranian intellectuals and social theorists who view *1968 Event* as the turning-point without realizing that this year may be of significance for eurocentric social sciences and societies. In other words, we tend to forget that every society may have its own turning-points and it is wrong to assume that "1968" is the criterion for all global changes. This mode of viewing global issues is what one could term as "House Negro-Mentality" in the sense Malcolm X conceptualized it, i.e. one who associates himself with the "master-narrative" in a way that he denies his own subjectivity by becoming one with the eurocentric vision of the world. Malcolm X presents another turning-point in historiographical sense and for him the year 1964 is when the worldwide revolution of the oppressed people took place (1966. 49). Malcolm X argues that

> 1964 will see the Negro revolt evolve and merge into the worldwide black revolution that has been taking place on this earth. . . . The so-called revolt will become a real black revolution. Now the black revolution has been taking place in Africa and Asia and Latin America; when I say black, I mean non-white—black, brown, red or yellow. Our brothers and sisters in Asia, who were colonized by the Europeans, our brothers and sisters in Asia, who were colonized by the Europeans, and in Latin America, the peasants, who were colonized by the Europeans, have been involved in a struggle . . . to get the colonialists . . . off their land. . . . And there is no system on this earth which has proven itself more corrupt, more criminal, than this

system that in 1964 still colonizes 22 million African-American, still enslaves 22 million Afro-Americans (1966. 49–50).

To put it bluntly, for Rojas the symbolic year is 1968 when "that great rupturing—event—occurred" (Rojas, 2004. 197) but for Malcolm X the rupturing event is 1964 when the black people shook off their yoke in America and looked for "freedom, justice, equality" (1966. 51) and refused to be considered as a colonized community (1966. 50) within America. In other words, the turning-point for Malcolm X differs surely from Rojas' perspective and this would clearly have fundamental bearings upon their respective frames of their social theory. In the eurocentric historiography

> It is clear that the fundamental dividing circumstance of 1968 has spread on a worldwide scale. And it is now also clear that—way and beyond its multiple and diverse forms of expression at the different geographic spots, obviously associated with the historic features of each respective region, nation or space—, the 1968 movement is deep-down (basically) a true cultural revolution. Consequently, at its most representative and characteristic epicenters as well as at the entire group of places and spaces of its multiple appearances, the historical 1968 rupture always emerges with a double scenario: one, as a process in which the explanation is never entirely complete stemming only from the data of the corresponding local situation—forwarding us therefore to its universal dimension—and the other, also as a transformation in which, whatever might be the political fate or the mediate or immediate destiny of its direct actors, as individuals or collectively, it always ends up by radically upsetting, without any possibility of turning back, the forms of functioning and of reproduction of the main cultural structures that it refutes and questions (Rojas, 2004. 197–8).

For Malcolm X seems the history is conceived in a different fashion as instead of 1968, it is the significance of 1964 which is symbolized in his narrative, i.e. it has the possibility of having a "world-wide [consequences] . . . on this earth" (X, 1966. 49–50).

This creates a different mindset and based on this symbolic difference the subjectivity which is developed within the parameters of Malcolm X's point of departure would surely generate other sets of turning-points. Although it is undeniable that we may be able to find common grounds as the objective is freedom, justice and equality in all truly humanistic traditions which are neither integrationist nor separationist but recognitionist, i.e. "fighting for the right to live as free humans in . . . society" (X, 1966. 51). These are the ideals which Rojas discerns in the 1968 revolt by arguing that

> History is not an automatic process with is inevitably one way, but rather it is a process carried out by men themselves, who with our collective action and our reflections help to decide their possible destinies, in accordance with the conditions of possibility of each specific historic moment (2004. 214).

REVOLUTION AND RADICAL MEANS OF POLITICAL TRANSFORMATION

No doubt that Malcolm X is a revolutionary thinker and it is wrong to define his body of knowledge within the narrow boundaries of disciplinary academia. In other words, his mode of sociological imagination bears no resemblance to what Allama Jafari terms as *clerkish mentalité in human sciences* (Miri, 2014. 58). This is to argue that he symbolizes a type of thinker which I would like to conceptualize as a *street thinker*. What does this concept mean? I can explain this by a brief reference to sport terminology which would enable us to comprehend the concept of the "street thinker" in a better fashion. I am sure all of you are familiar with boxing more or less. In boxing field, the experts talk about two kinds of boxing styles, i.e. the professional boxing and the street fight boxing. The skills which a boxer may learn in the boxing clubs are very useful but when one steps outside the ring the techniques which have been adopted inside the ring they should be modified to fit the new environment. Otherwise one may get beaten by harsh realities of fighting which are ongoing in violent streets of our cities. If this comparison is permitted then I would draw your attention to the fact that academic social thinkers look similar to professional boxers who are trained within specific parameters of academia and their particular styles do obstruct the transmissions of realities which they intend to study and understand. In other words, the type of encounter which Malcolm X portrays in his lifework demonstrates a profound affinity to the models of *street fighting* where the fighters do not use gloves and come in touch with harsh realities in bare forms. To put it differently, the position through which Malcolm X approached social problems were the violent streets of Bronx and Manhattan which were fundamentally in contradiction to ivory towers of Harvard or Princeton. Isn't perspective everything? How does our perspective emerge? Isn't biography pivotal in the constitution of our perspective? Some may argue that everything we see is a perspective, not the truth, i.e. the way we gain insight about life is not separated from where we are positioned in society and the world. Said differently, in the matrix of Malcolm X's social theory, I discern a model of intellectual engagement which is more suited to realities of the 21st century where academia as a symbolic world of learning has lost its integrity as well as sovereignty due to its marriage with corporate knights. Malcolm X presents the concerns of streets and embodies the spirit of streets in a world which have lost the spirit of *caring engagement* with the other.

Now let me get back to the question of revolution and how Malcolm X understood the "real revolution" as it seems he believed that we could orchestrate certain political changes and sell it as revolution to oppressed groups or people in any society. In other words, Malcolm X argued that a real revolution involves systemic transformation which would create a *free*, *just*, and *equal* social context for all citizens who happen to live in a particular political order (1966. 50). The core of revolution in Malcolm X's discourse is interconnected to the question of "Land." Because the model he has in mind is related to the experiences of non-whites around the globe who has lost their lands and have been turned into refugees in their own homelands such as Palestinians and South Africans respectively under the governments of Zionist regime or ex-Apartheid regime of South Africa. In other words, displacement brought about by Colonialism lied at the heart of Malcolm X's notion of revolution which could not be dissociated from the question of "Land." Once you lose your land you turn into a tenant and being a tenant could have grave consequences for the patterns of group mentality in strict political sense of the term. In addition, we should add the racial dimension into Malcolm X's perception of the "other" which was deeply interwoven with the historical trauma of slavery as far as the Afro-Americans are concerned. To put it differently, Malcolm X was not looking for a simple regime-change in America. On the contrary, he was looking for colossal changes which would not only liberate blacks from their historical negritude traumas but also emancipate white people from their alienating inhumanity. But these changes are not possible through merely political decrees which do not touch the hearts of people in truly existential sense of the term. At any rate, the concept of revolution is "always based on land" (1966. 50). But it is wrong to assume that one can get back the land through negotiation because the land is where the identity is constructed upon and once you lose your land you lose your sense of being someone or losing your sense of belonging – and the one who has robbed your land surely has robbed your sense of identity before that he has taken the physical territories where you used to reside. In other words, Malcolm X's insistence upon land was an attempt to carve a sense of identity in the symbolic universe in America and when he realized that this is not possible then he struggled for separation. Of course, he oscillated between various positions depending on different scenarios which appeared before him during turbulent years of the Cold War in US.

However, Malcolm believed that what has been taken cannot be returned peacefully and a revolution "is never based on begging somebody for an integrated cup of coffee" (1966. 50). Maybe it is useful to mention that he was the master of figurative form of speech as he was deeply well-versed in the Holy Scriptures in an unprecedented fashion which is rarely seen in other social theorists of his caliber. What does he mean by an integrated cup of coffee in relation to the revolutionary sentiment? In order to understand Malcolm X's symbolic language we need to get a picture of the American society during the racial revolution which led to the assassination of Malcolm X in Harlem on February 21, 1965. There are different narratives about the racial question in America but the one which Malcolm X relates seems to be different than the mainstream accounts. In his view, the black movement was derailed from its primary objectives by a complex plot which was designed by influential power elites who brought John F. Kennedy into the White House. Malcolm X relates the story in the following fashion, i.e.

> Roy Wilkins attacked King; . . . they accused King and Congress of Racial Equality of raising all the money and not paying it back. This happened; I've got it in documented evidence. . . . Roy started attacking King, and King started attacking Roy, and Farmer started attacking both. And as these Negroes of national stature began to attack each other, they began to lose their control of the Negro masses. The Negroes were out in the streets. They were talking about how they were going to march on Washington. Right at that time Birmingham had exploded. They began to stab the crackers in the back and bust them up. . . . That's when Kennedy sent in the troops, . . . and said "this is a moral issue." They even said they were going out to the airport and lay down on the runway and not let any airplanes land. That was revolution. That was the black revolution. It was the grass

roots out there in the street. It scared the white man to death, scared the white power structure in Washington, D. C., to death; they called Wilkins, they called in Randolph, they called in these national Negro leaders that you respect and told them, "Call it off." Kennedy said, "Look, you all are letting this thing go too far." And Old Tom said, "Boss, I can't stop it, because I did not start it." They said, "I'm not even in it, much less at the head of it." They said, "These Negroes are doing things on their own. They're running ahead of us." And that old shrewd fox, he said, "If you all aren't in it, I'll put you in it." They had a meeting at the Carlyle Hotel in New York City. The Carlyle Hotel is owned by the Kennedy Family. A philanthropic society headed by a white man called all the top civil-rights leaders to gather at the Carlyle Hotel. And he told them, "By you all fighting each other, you are destroying the civil-rights movement. And since you're fighting over money from white liberals, let us set what is known as the Council for the United Civil Rights Leadership. Let's form this council, and all the civil-rights organizations will belong to it, and we'll use it for fund-raising purposes." A million and a half dollars—split up between leaders that you have been following, going to jail for, crying crocodile tears for. And they're nothing but Frank James and Jesse James and the what-do-you-call-'em brothers. As soon as they got the setup organized, the white man made available to them top public-relations experts; opened the new media across the country at their disposal, which then began to project these Big Six as the leaders of the march. Originally they weren't even in the march. The same white element that put Kennedy into power—labor, the Catholics, the Jews, and liberal Protestants; the same clique that put Kennedy in power, joined the march on Washington. (1966. 14–16)

This is the narrative which Malcolm X depicts about the background contours of the Black Movement which evolved into the Black Revolution but gradually was infiltrated and finally hijacked by powerful elements of the *White Ancien Régime* . It is in this context that Malcolm X uses a figurative language to explain how authentic social movements lose their political objectives and turn, instead, into reactionary hooliganistic gangs without any progressive political objectives. To highlight this point, Malcolm X argues that the *White Ancien Régime* uses the coffee and cream policy to derail authentic oppositions to the capitalist world system both within and without America. What is the coffee and cream policy? It's just

> Like when you've got some coffee that's too black, which means it's too strong. What do you do? You integrate it with cream, you make it weak. But if you pour too much cream in it, you won't even know you ever had coffee. It used to be hot, it becomes cool. It used to be strong, it becomes weak. It used to wake you up, now it puts you to sleep. This is what they did with the march on Washington. They joined it. They did not integrate it, they infiltrated it. They joined it, became a part of it, took it over. And as they took it over, it lost its militancy. It ceased to be angry, it ceased to be hot, it ceased to be uncompromising. Why, it ceased to be a march. It became a picnic, a circus. Nothing but a circus, with clowns and all (1966. 16).

In other words, Malcolm X seems to believe that within the context of capitalism authentic revolutions are not possible unless revolutionary groups breed a sense of militancy within their body of praxis. If not then the power elites in the capitalist system would take over and change the course of emancipative movements by the policy of integrating coffee and cream. His model of revolution could be employed in contexts such as the one between Israel and Palestine where the latter has lost her land and the other using the policy of integrating coffee and cream. If Malcolm X was alive he would surely have argued against those who encourage Palestinians to turn "the other cheek" (1966. 50). In other words, he would have argued that revolution is

> Never based on begging somebody for an integrated cup of coffee. Revolutions are never fought turning the other cheek.

> Revolutions are never based upon love-your-enemy and pray-for-those-who-spitefully-use-you. And revolutions are never waged singing "We Shall Overcome" (1966. 50).

On the contrary, Malcolm X believed that revolutions

> Are based upon bloodshed. Revolutions are never compromising. Revolutions are never based upon negotiations. Revolutions are never based upon any kind of tokenism whatsoever. Revolutions are never even based upon that which is begging a corrupt system to accept us into it. Revolutions overturn systems (1966. 50).

This is to argue that structural changes should occur but these transformations should not be only confined to external structures. On the contrary, the structures which make up the contours of human mindsets should be transformed too. Otherwise, the corrupt system would reform itself upon the patterns of the old Ancien Régime which deprives people from their inalienable rights as human beings.

Chapter Four

The Epic of America

THE MYSTERY OF UNSAID

Before pondering upon the mysteries of the *unsaid*, it should be clarified what the *unsaid* does not stand for. In other words, the unsaid should not be understood as the "not said" in a verbal sense of the term, i.e. what is not expressed or uttered out loud. The unsaid stands for possibilities which are not possible to be realized in "love-your-enemy" or "by turning the other cheek" form of social praxis (X, 1966. 50). It is well-known that what is left unsaid is often more powerful and poetic but here the core of "unsaid" is assumed in terms of "verbal statement" which is kept linguistically implicit in the matrix of a sentence. But the *unsaid* which I have in mind is related to range of possibilities which are potentially felt in the hearts but inaccessible to minds due to modalities which reign supreme in a given social/cultural/civilizational form. Who can break modalities which fashion how we are at a given time in a particular society? This is a question which one can read between the lines of speeches which Malcolm X left as an intellectual legacy for everyone who is interested in the power of possibilities or the relation between poetry and politics. In other words, poetry and politics share common ground when it comes to potential, promise and redress, as suggested by the adage: *We campaign in poetry, but govern in prose*. In so far as explicit communication is the tip of the iceberg, implication is its submerged under-structure: unsaid, often unseen, potentially lethal yet at times unutterably beautiful. From equivocation to consideration, from persuasion to in-group consolidation, from threat to thrall, unsaid plays an important role not only in politics, but in life itself. We have a choice either to master the unsaid or to be mastered by it as this is a choice between living under emancipative possibilities or authoritarian thralldoms.

In 1978 Stephen A. Tyler published his *The Said and the Unsaid* where he talked about the relation between the climates of ideas and the subjective dimensions of human understanding as well as the key locus of meaning in the constitution of self and society. By meaning, he referred to the possibility of relationality which could be realized in a given society at a particular epoch. In other words, it was assumed that everything could not be said due to the limitability of relationality at a given time in history which could obstruct the eruptions of all possibilities within the boundaries of possible realities. This could be understood in an oppositional fashion by reference to impossibility of possibilities within human realm of social relationships. This is to argue that society is a possibility but possibilities within the parameters of a given society are not always in favor of realizing all possible possibilities at simultaneous realm of temporality-cum-spatiality. To put it differently, a possibility within a certain social context could entail the impossibility of another breakthrough. For instance, racism in a given society is a possibility which in its full realization would mean that egalitarianism would never be a possibility in that given society and one should categorize it as an impossible possibility. But an impossible possibility is still a possibility due to the fact that human reality is fashioned in terms of autonomy and determinism, i.e. human realities are series of occurrences which unfold through free forms of agency and determined norms of structures. This is to state that one reality may not be possible in a given epoch but as long as it is even an impossible possibility then it could have revolutionizing effects upon actual universe of realities. This is what I term the *mystery of unsaid* which could be occasionally realized by very extra-ordinary intellectuals. These types of intellectuals could change the rules of the game because they are not schooled in the art of ordinary techniques which rule supreme in every epoch. They seem to be illiterate about the ordinary frame of actions and this mode of being create a sense of extra-ordinariness in them which have far-reaching consequences for the makeup of reality, meaning, mentalité and culture. When *unsaid* is *said* creativity bursts into reality and the outburst will transform the parameters of reality in a fundamental fashion. For instance, in a time when America was in the middle of the Cold War with USSR and the threat perception was real, Malcolm X talked about things which even the most imaginative sociologists of US did not dare to think about even in their most private recesses of their hearts, let alone formulate them publicly. But Malcolm X dared and his daring mode of being brought him to a position of expressing the *unsaid* as an impossible possibility and this brought American society into a new epoch as though somebody from the world beyond kicked the white society into an impossible possibility. When we compare the giants of social theory in America we cannot find any equal to Malcolm X as far as the *sociology of the unsaid* is concerned as he is one of the rare souls who expressed the *unsaid* in a *said* fashion. If I would try to find a contemporary equal to Malcolm X in the 20th century I cannot but choose Ali Shariati from Iran who is one of the founders of *unsaid* social theory. Both of them lived very short lives but they impacted their respective societies and the global society in quite similar fashions and ironically they seem to share many common grounds which have not been studied yet. However, when the unsaid is said then the perceived reality which was bearable for whatever reasons then it could not be perceived in the same fashion anymore and one can witness cracks everywhere in every corner of any given society at any given time. When Malcolm X was talking about "separation" from the white America he was unequivocally challenging the system and declaring outright war on white masters. Surely he knew that this is not a battle which could be won militarily but it is certain that he was looking for a total destruction of house-negro mentality which was inherited from slavery. Although physical slavery was abolished in the 19th century but Malcolm could see the manifestations of mental enslavement everywhere among Afro-Americans. When he expressed the unsaid yokes were shattered in the minds of the white rulers but the said came to realization six decades later by the appearance of Barack Hussein Obama in the White House. However, if Malcolm X was here today he would have cautioned everyone about the integrating policy of coffee and cream as the oppressive custodians of the *said* would not leave peacefully the ground for the realization of the emancipative forces of the *unsaid*.

RACISM AND AMERICAN FOREIGN POLICY

I have never seen any contemporary social theorist who makes a direct correlation between the American domestic policy and America's foreign policy by arguing that the latter is an extension of the former which is based on "racial segregationism." In other words, Malcolm X is one of the rare contemporary social thinkers who argues forcefully that the American political structure is based on racism which "controls America's foreign policy" (1966. 57) too. This is to argue that the world system which is checked and balanced by America is racially-motivated and Malcolm X is one of unusual thinkers who attempt to catalogue the strategies which govern the system. The social theory of Malcolm X could be studied through this point of departure and the outcomes would be of great important in various fields of social sciences such as "international relations" and "comparative political theories." For instance, how could we explain the "containment policy" of US against Iran or China? Is this only explainable through the logic of capitalism, strategy of hegemony or should one take into consideration the "racial element" in conceptualizing current scenarios in the world of politics? I think racism plays a significant role in world politics and it would be a great remiss if we disregard its pivotal role in the constitution of global strategies of hegemony.

ISLAM, RELIGION, AND THE QUESTION OF HERMENEUTICS

One of the serious questions which haunt Muslim mind today is the question of interpretation as there are various opposing groups which claim to have the "right interpretative frame of reference" over against the other rivals. In other words, the intellectual question of textual interpretation with philological dimensions has turned into a serious political battle where the warring opponents seek to obtain the means of legitimacy. This is to argue that the problem of textual philology has turned into the politics of text as the sacred text is not a matter of personal growth but sociopolitical governmentality in a religious canopy where hermeneutics is not the art of *vershten* but the means of exercising *authority*. This is an important question which should be taken into consideration when studying the *politics of scriptures* in Malcolm X's social theoretical paradigm. In other words, when we look at Malcolm X's view on religion and scripture we should have in mind a present concern along with the historical dilemma as both may not be of the similar nature. This is to argue when Malcolm X talks about Islam as a paradigm this insistence should be understood in reference to the White colonization of the Bible which did not leave any room for emancipative innovation for the oppressed black people in the context of America. But when we talk about the interpretative legacy of Malcolm X in the present context of global Islamism then we should take a different approach which is of a critical character vis-à-vis Malcolm X's position toward the question of religiosity or what is considered to be religion. To put it differently, while the position of Malcolm X is of emancipative nature toward the politics of scripture during the Black Revolution in 1964 but the same celebratory mode could not be attached to the consequences of his politics of religion in the 21st century. What do I mean by this statement? The politics of hermeneutics needs to be elaborated further as there are many stereotypes as far as scholarly approaches are concerned whenever researchers touch the question of religion in relation to what eurocentric scholars have concocted as "tradition."

Approaches to the study of Islam in America often discuss religious movements in America with reference to a dichotomy between the *secular* and the *religious* and consequently focus on conservative Islamic streams of thought that view these two concepts as inherently in conflict. This means that modernist and reformist strains of Islamic thought in America have been neglected in the scholarly literature, despite their immense importance to the history of Islam in the United States of America, in general, and in the formation of Malcolm X's perspective during the years which led to the Black Revolution of 1964, in particular.

It is no secret that the eurocentric discussion of religion, an analytic that holds in tension two supposedly dichotomous notions, the *religious* and the sec*u*lar, has been all-pervasive. As is well known, this dichotomy has been called into question by scholars who point to the mutual interdependence of these notions and their necessary intertwining, especially in the practice of what is conventionally deemed the secular or the religious (Asad 2003; Mahmood 2009). As Saba Mahmood points out,

> The religious and the secular are not so much immutable essences or opposed ideologies as they are concepts that gain a

particular salience with the emergence of the modern state and attendant politics—concepts that are, furthermore, interdependent and necessarily linked in their mutual transformation and historical emergence (2009: 836).

Asad and Mahmood's approaches imply that the secular and the religious are not mutually impermeable domains that continually vie for dominance in the public sphere; instead, they give meaning to each other. Negotiating their boundaries, and thus their mutual definition, is a major task of religious thought in the contemporary world. There is a temporal component to this ideological or political dichotomy between the religious and the secular: the traditional and the modern. As with the secular and the religious, these notions are often assumed to be immutably opposed, but it could be suggested that they in fact depend on each other, both historically and discursively. As Mahmood explains,

> Tradition . . . is not a set of symbols and idioms that justify present practices, neither is it an unchanging set of cultural prescriptions that stand in contrast to what is changing, contemporary, or modern. Nor is it a historically fixed social structure. Rather, the past is the very ground through which the subjectivity and self-understanding of a tradition's adherents are constituted (2005: 115).

Said differently, as a continuous hermeneutic engagement with previous discourses, religious "tradition" is the necessary ground of the religious believer's construction of her own sense of agency or participation in a particular religious community. Tradition is not simply the static "other" of modernity. Nor does it have to be identified with conservatism: if tradition is the medium through which a participant interacts with her faith tradition, as Mahmood suggests, it may be interpreted in any number of different ways and utilized for any number of different projects. For instance, certain uses of tradition may authorize socially conservative patriarchal gender roles, while others may undermine these and be employed in emancipative fashions to combat deeply racially segregated political orders.

In America the study of Malcolm X has not moved beyond the questions of race and in so doing most scholars have got focused, as far as religion is concerned, on the dichotomy of secularity and religiosity. In other words, in the study of Islamic thought in relation to Malcolm X, there has been a prevailing focus on conservative groups (such as the Nation of Islam) or thinkers (e.g. Elijah Mohammad) who see tradition as a means to negotiate the boundaries between the white community as well as the secular and the black community as well as the religious in the public sphere in favor of the latter. However, the complex relationship between the secular and the religious suggests that there are other possible configurations of the boundaries between the secular and the religious and other possible uses of tradition in negotiating these boundaries.

Having said this, we need to look at the other aspects of religion which may have had an impact on Malcolm X's perspective on religion too. It is a very well-established fact that Malcolm X was raised by a Baptist minister so we know that Christianity exerted a powerful influence on his early life. It wasn't until Malcolm served a seven-year prison sentence that he converted to the Nation of Islam. In other words, it may seem justifiable to reconfigure the politics of Bible in the constitution of Malcolm X's view on religion and the ways in which it could be employed in mobilizing the masses. Because when he left the Nation of Islam, he did not stop believing in religion and more importantly he started to take the social dimensions of religiosity more seriously as this could be corroborated by reference to his dedication in establishing the Muslim Organization in America. After his long international travels, Malcolm X founded a new Muslim organization called Muslim Mosque, Inc., which sought to mobilize Muslims and non-Muslims alike to the cause of black equality. In other words, we need to understand his conversion from Christianity to Islam and also his transformation from the Nation of Islam to Islam as a socio-political worldview and more importantly the paradigm-shift of Malcolm X from being at the *service of religion* into a view of religion that considers it at the *service of humanity*, i.e. the authoritarian model versus emancipative model of religiosity. In the current studies on Malcolm X, I have not seen any of these problematizations and the potentials of his social theoretical concepts have been deeply undertheorized. It seems the undertheorization of Malcolm X is not only of intellectual nature but I think there are other issues which have inhibited scholars to work on him in a more appropriate fashion that his work deserves. In other words, there are widespread myths or sentimental reasons which could explain the undertheorization of Malcolm X's social theory. For instance, the dominant view that Malcolm X spent the bulk of his life as an activist on the fringe of society; the constructed view that Malcolm X was too extreme and his extremism put many off and discouraged many to take him seriously; the endorsed official opinion which attempted to portray Malcolm X as a phony in comparison to Martin Luther King; and finally the mainstream white view which seemed to construct an irrational image of Malcolm X in comparison to King who appeared, only appeared, to be more reasonable and rational. Certainly there are many other myths which have been instrumental in regard to undertheorization of Malcolm X's social theory but I think these few would give us a good lead to explore the problem in more detailed fashions.

The question which needs to be addressed is the role of Bible in the constitution of Malcolm X's social theology. When we look at the Bible there seems to be no room for racist justification as according to the Bible, Adam and Eve were of one *flesh*. Thus, no other Races were created in the Garden of Eden. But the history of the Holy Scriptures seems to demonstrate a different saga. In 1452

Pope Nicholas V penned his "Papal Bull" known as the "Dum Diversas"

> We grant you [Kings of Spain and Portugal] by these present documents, with our Apostolic Authority, full and free permission to invade, search out, capture, and subjugate the Saracens and pagans and any other unbelievers and enemies of Christ wherever they may be, as well as their kingdoms, duchies, counties, principalities, and other property [. . .] and to reduce their persons into perpetual slavery. (Nicholas, 2013)

In other words, it is impossible to understand Christianity in America without problematizting the concept of "Perpetual Slavery" which was used as the cornerstone of modern institutions in America for more than 400 years. Malcolm X was born into a reality where even the God of the White people sanctioned the colored people to be enslaved and their person reduced "into perpetual slavery" (Nicholas, 2013). To put it differently, the Bible was used to consolidate the systematic racism in its total institutionalized form in America in a fashion unprecedented in the entire human history. This is to argue that the politics of Islam needs to be understood in relation to white-interpretation of the Bible which caused Malcolm X to provide a different sacrosanct frame of reference in a context where the God seemed to have a white color. Malcolm X knew very well that the Black Mentalité is deeply religious and it is futile to force upon it a socialistic position which suited few highly eccentric thinkers in Black Ivory Towers of the post-World War II.

To put it differently, in a context where God seems to side with the oppressors then one should find another God who can bless you in your just struggle. It is in this milieu that we should understand the position Malcolm X takes on religion, in general, and Islam, in particular. What is Islam? This is a simple but a fundamental question which forces itself upon anyone who is not a "House Intellectual" and also is looking to go beyond simplistic interpretations of religion and religiosity which are byproducts of secularism and house intellectual mentality. Malcolm X, both as a social theorist and as a "Field Intellectual" embarks upon this path by defining what he considers as the true spirit of Islam and how he defines the true/prophetic mission of Islam in the contemporary world. In his *Nigerian Epistle* he argues that *"Islam is a religion which concerns itself with the human rights of all mankind . . . , despite race, color, or creed. It recognizes all . . . as part of one human family"* (1966. 61). Here in this brief quote one could see that Islam is the religion which is in favor of equality and it is only Islam which could remove the apparent and latent traces of racism in the White American Social Order and societies where "race" is an issue. Because in Malcolm X's view, Islam is based on the familial conception of humanity and once you submit to its principles, you *"also . . . automatically . . . accept each other . . . as brothers and sisters, regardless . . . of differences in . . . complexion"* (1966. 60).

Although this position could be acceptable but I think there are certain points which should be taken into consideration as the *familial conception of humanity* is not unique to Islam. In other words, we can even find this notion in Christianity and Judaism so this cannot explain Malcolm X's hermeneutic position on religion. It seems the question is not only of theological nature which one could solve by reference to passages of the Holy Scriptures in the ways fundamentalist exegetes of various religious traditions attempt to achieve legitimacy over against their rivals. On the contrary, the problem lies in the ways in which the Scriptures have been appropriated in different social settings by distinct groups in human societies which fashion existential modes of being of men and women in the paradoxical contexts of the everyday life. When Malcolm X is a witness to the assassination of his father who was a Christian minister at the hands of the Black Legion which adhered to a Biblical interpretation of racism and violence against the colored people then surely he would have searched for a way out of this world where even God and Czar sanction your perpetual annihilation. But the hermeneutics strategy of Malcolm X could create problems if it is taken as it is formulated. In other words, in a context where there are different strategies of religious hermeneutics then simple reference to verses of the Holy Scriptures without taking into consideration the social models which have shaped our experiences of politics of Islam is, to say the least, a naïve approach. It is true that Islam is a religion of peace but this peaceful religion is shaping the experiences of others in a violent fashion and the peacefulness cannot solely be measured in reference to one's own self. On the contrary, peacefulness is a relational concept which could be realized when the wholly other is receiving peaceful treatment of the one who claims to follow a peaceful worldview. In other words, we need to take the politics of hermeneutics very seriously as one of the reasons that compelled Malcolm X toward religious conversion was the oppressive strategies of Christianity which was materialized in various dimensions of social institutions in America during his lifetime. Today the same thing may happen to Islam in a global scale as the everyday experiences of people in relation to Islam is in favor of authoritarian interpretations. To put it differently, it is very dangerous when in the heart of people God and Czar seem to be in the same bed as this symbolic reality forced Malcolm X to distance from dominant religious symbolism of the White America and today the same thing may happen for people who see in Islam an image of "Perpetual Violence." One may argue that this is not the essence of Islam but the question is not of essential significance. On the contrary, it is the existential experiences which could transform the rules of the game as the politics of Malcolm X's hermeneutics strategy demonstrated in the context of America. For instance, on the eve of the Iranian Revolution in 1979, even one single verse of the Holy Scripture could incite the masses to create heroic scenes but today the situation is different. There is a public apathy toward anything related to religion. Why is it so? The essence of religion has not changed but the everyday experiences of religiosity or oppressive strategies of religiosity and politics of hermeneutics have changed the attitudes of people toward the symbolic universe of religion. In this context, people look for a different kind of god but this time the god may not be the type of deity that the Czars are looking for.

GOOD SOCIETY

Every great social theorist has a philosophy of *Good Society*. In other words, any serious social theorist is seeking after apposite principles of reality on which s/he could establish her/his theoretical assumptions or what is better known as normative dimensions of any sound social theory. Malcolm X is no exception in this regard as he wrestled with these questions during his short but creative intellectual life. But the important question for any creative social theorist is not only reflections upon permanent principles which govern the immutable patterns of communal human reality in its metaphysical sense or even mere analysis of realities of a given society without taking into consideration the normative principles of human existence. In other words, critical social theorists are those types of thinkers who are able to establish dialogical connections between conflicting realms of *isness* and *ought-to-be*. This is to argue that Malcolm X was able to make this dialogical connection between the realities of the existing American society and immutable principles of the Good Society which should be the goal of any sane community by realizing its ideals. Otherwise, the society we live in would turn into an "Iron Cage" which would reduce the being of humanity into a necrophilic set of alienating social relations without any room for self-actualization and inspiring communal interactions. Malcolm X does not define the parameters of the "Good Society" which he has in mind but uses a figurative language in elaborating the shortcomings of the racially-stricken capitalist system of America. He argues that every system has its own limits even the most advanced social organizations are still human organizations and by definition are limited. Of course, the question is not that how we can establish a limitless social organization on this planet as it was desired by fathers of modern ideologies who had a deep contempt against religions. On the contrary, the nodal point of this problematique is how we are able to establish a society where the involuntary limits on its members could be checked and balanced. Malcolm X is of the opinion that the American racist social order is unable to deliver its promises or what is publicly known as the parameters of the American Dream, namely a set of ideals in which freedom includes the opportunity for prosperity and success, and an upward social mobility achieved through hard work. Why did Malcolm X disagree with these beautiful ideals which were known as *The Epic of America*? In 1931 when James Truslow Adams attempted to define the American Dream by arguing that the life should be better and richer and fuller for everyone, with opportunity for each according to ability or achievement regardless of social class or circumstances of birth (Adams, 1931), Malcolm X lost startlingly his father on the same year that Adams published his book, i.e. 1931 at the hands of the White Supremacist Group of the Black Legion in Lansing, Michigan. In other words, the American Dream was perceived by public intellectuals such as Malcolm X as a deeply white dream by arguing that

> I'm not an American. I'm one of the 22 million black people who are the victims of Americanism. One of the 22 million black people . . . who are the victims of democracy, nothing but disguised . . . hypocrisy. So, I'm not standing here speaking to you as an American, or a patriot, or a flag-saluter, or a flag-waver—no, not I. I'm speaking as a victim of this American system. And I see America through the eyes of the victim. I don't see any American dream; I see an American nightmare" (1966. 26).

What Adams viewed as the epic of America or the parameters of the American Dream, it came to be associated by Malcolm X as an American Nightmare. In the collective mind of the black people there were no rooms for freedom, social mobility or success. On the contrary, deep in their hearts they felt as victims and did not share the ideals of the White House which represented the political aspirations of the White American. In other words, Malcolm X believed that the contradiction in the racist social order is not an accident but it is inherent to the system which cannot be but discriminatory, oppressive, segregationist, exploitative and inhumane. He argued that

> It's impossible for a chicken to produce a duck egg—even though they both belong to the same family of fowl. A chicken just doesn't have it within its system to produce a duck egg. It can't do it. It can only produce according to what that particular system was constructed to produce (1966. 68).

In other words, the racial system of American social order can only produce according to racial considerations which are built upon division of races and the supremacy of the white race. This is to argue that Malcolm X used the metaphor of "fowl" in relation to the social systems which are not favorable to freedom, liberty, equality, and fraternity by arguing that the

> [capitalist] ... system ... cannot produce freedom. ... It is impossible for this system, this economic system, this political system, this social system ... to produce freedom, ... [equality, fraternity and liberty]. ... [Because the system is based on] ... oppression, exploitation, degradation, segregation and humiliation ... [as it is] ... impossible [for] a chicken [to] produce a duck egg ... [it is also] ... impossible for this system to produce [and materialize] ... [the ideals of good society which are epitomized in slogans of the French Revolution] (1966. 67-9).

In other words, for Malcolm X the "American System" is not the example of the *Good Society* but it is, as a matter of fact, a new type of colonialism. Although this may not be a novel idea today but six decades ago this was a revolutionary notion coming from a Black political activist who opposed the American Dream by demonstrating that it is a white dream rather than a humane ideal for everyone who aspired to participate in realization of *sane ideals*. Further, he argued that European colonialism has run into a new course which is represented by America. But the interesting aspect of Malcolm X's approach is how he conceptualizes the American racist imperialism. He argues that the colonial mode of American racism is best conceptualized as "American Dollarism." This is a very interesting concept in explaining the racist nature of American neo-colonial system which in Ander Gunder Frank's parlance is termed as "Paper Tiger." In Malcolm X's own words, it's

> Easy to become a satellite today without even being aware of it. This country can seduce God. Yes, it has that seductive power—the power of dollarism. You can cuss out colonialism, imperialism and all other kinds of isms, but it's hard for you to cuss that dollarism. When they drop those dollars on you, your soul goes (1966. 199).

To put it differently, dollarism is another concept for the necrophilic feature which has enveloped all dimensions and realms of human society today. The seductive power of cash-nexus or what Malcolm X conceptualizes as the "power of dollarism" (1966. 199) has created a set social trait which is shared by

> Millions of people [who] share the same vices [which make them unable] to attain freedom, spontaneity, and a genuine expression of self [and this is a] socially patterned defect [which is produced in the matrix of American Dollarism] (Fromm, 1955. 15).

THE PROPHETIC AND THE ANALYTIC

In academia, we have grown accustom to believe that the prime duty of a sociologist is to strive to be disinterested, in the sense of not letting immediate political sympathies get in the way of describing or explaining "how things are." In other words, objectivity is an ideal that has shaped the background assumptions of disciplinary social theory. Although objectivity is intrinsically an important issue within the context of sociological theory but the ways in which it has been constructed in disciplinary social sciences seems to be a little old-fashioned. For example, a committed sociological theory such as Islamism is strongly governed by anti-eurocentric values, but its claims are still "objective" and even "factual" in character: that eurocentrism exists and that is systematically favors the interest of western institutions, for example. However, the image of academic as a disinterested person is related to the self-image of the sociologist as a *scientist* which involves resisting the temptation to go completely postmodern and postcolonial, i.e. to defend aspects of the Western intellectual heritage stemming from the Enlightenment by continuing to think that the sociologist is really a scientist. But the other side of this defensive strategy has been the total negligence toward serious political issues which have to do with the oppressive state of capitalist social order such as systematic racism. At any rate, this is not the only self-image which social theory had about itself. The revolutionary image is a more popular view of the purpose of sociology which was adopted by many people in 1960 and 1970 when in a world so obviously full of inequality and exploitation, the "scientific" image of the sociology was a dismal abdication of moral consciousness—a cop-out. It is in this context that the discourse of Malcolm X was born but the American academia resisted so forcefully that his message would not enter the classrooms across the United States of America while he was alive. Indeed, the very idea that social science could be "above" the clash of political movements, or that it could be "value-free" in its consequences, was rejected as being part of the dominant ideology of the Western, capitalist, racist and patriarchal system. In other words, the discourse of Malcolm X could be conceptualized within the parameters of emancipatory image of social theory, i.e. sociologist as someone who has to get off the fence and throw in his efforts with emancipatory movements. Although this is a powerful image but it seems academics having more and more trouble to associate with this type after the end of the Cold War. In other words, in the world of the post-Cold era, the image of the sociologist as a *professional*, rather than as a scientist or a revolutionary has strongly come to the fore. Some argue that in a situation in which students' families pay hefty fees for their education, and where there is a very competitive market for jobs and careers, both the ideal of a pure analyst and that of a world-transforming activist, could be regarded as a little lavish or even escapist. This change in the image has been very instrumental in disengagement strategies which have been operating in academia against appropriation of Malcolm X in the temple of sociology.

These three self-images of the sociologist could assist us in conceptualizing the typology of Malcolm X. In other words, what type of theorist is Malcolm X? Is he more of a scientist, revolutionary or professional? By a cursory look at the biography of Malcolm X one could readily realize that he had never been a professional theorist within the walls of mainstream academia. Although he cannot be considered as a scientist but there is an aspect in the notion of science which should be cherished and I think Malcolm X had it in his outlook during his entire life as a public intellectual. What is exactly that particular aspect which one can discover in Malcolm X? I think that is what I term as the "analytic power," i.e. the ability to discern objectively "what's going on" or explain "how things are." Malcolm had this ability and fused it with another ability which I term the "prophetic power" which is missing entirely in the context of *professional era*. There are ample references in Malcolm

X which could clearly demonstrate how he realized these two ideals in his outlook during the Black Revolution in America. During the election which led to the triumph of Kennedy over against Nixon, Malcolm X delivered a lecture on April 3, 1964 entitled *The Ballot or the Bullet*. The prose itself is a testimony to the genius of the man who could bring such an exhilarating mode to the public. But the content is deeply analytical and objective to the point that one thinks Malcolm X has masterminded the election campaign of the two candidates in 1960. Let me give you a glimpse of how he combined the two voices of the analytic and the prophetic in his speech on April 3, 1964. He believed that the only way the black people could unshackle the four hundred years of slavery in America is to gain awareness, political maturity and cultural integrity. He analyzed the situation which led to the triumph of J. F. Kennedy in 1960 presidential election in the following fashion, i.e. the eyes of the 22 million black people

> Are coming open. They're beginning to see what they used to only look at. They're becoming politically mature. They are realizing that there are new political trends from coast to coast. As they see these new political trends, it's possible for them to see that every time there's an election the races are so close that they have to have a recount. They had to recount in Massachusetts to see who was going to be governor, it was so close. It was the same way in Rhode Island, in Minnesota, and in many other parts of the country. And the same with Kennedy and Nixon when they ran for president. It was so close they had to count all over again. Well, what does that mean? It means that when white people are evenly divided, and black people have a bloc of votes of their own, it is left up to them to determine who's going to sit in the White House and who's going to be in the dog house. It was the black man's vote that put the present administration in Washington, D. C. (X, 1966. 26).

Here we can see the voice of the analyst in Malcolm X who attempts to analyze the complex nuances of the rapidly changing political culture in America. But he does not stop at this point as he is not a disinterested scientist who is looking for objective ideals in a value-free fashion. On the contrary, he puts on the mantle of the prophet by urging people to take in their own hands their collective destiny before it is too late. He incites people by saying that

> Your vote, your dumb vote, your ignorant vote, your wasted vote put in an administration in Washington, D. C., that has seen fit to pass every kind of legislation imaginable, saving you until last, then filibustering on top of that. And your and my leaders have the audacity to run around clapping their hands and talk about how much progress we're making. And what a good president we have. If he wasn't good in Texas, he sure can't be good in Washington, D. C. Because Texas is a lynch state. It is in the same breath as Mississippi, no different; only they lynch you in Texas with a Texas accent and lynch you in Mississippi with a Mississippi accent. And these Negro leaders have the audacity to go and have dome coffee in the White House with a Texan, a Southern cracker—that's all he is—and then come out and tell you and me that he's going to be better for us because, since he's from the South, he knows how to deal with the Southerners. What kind of logic is that? Let Eastland be president, he's from the South too. He should be better able to deal with them than Johnson. Last but not least, I must say this concerning the great controversy over rifles and shotguns. Don't go out shooting people, but any time, brothers and sisters, and especially the men in this audience—some of you wearing Congressional Medals of Honor, with shoulders this wife, chests this big, muscles that big—any time you and I sit around and read where they bomb a church and murder in cold blood, not some grownups, but four little girls while they were praying to the same god the white man taught them to pray to, and you and I see the government go down and can't find who did it. Why, this man—he can find Eichmann hiding down in Argentina somewhere. Let two or three American soldiers, who are minding somebody else's business way over in South Vietnam, get killed, and he'll send battleships, sticking his nose in their business. He wanted to send troops down to Cuba and make them have what he calls

free elections—this old cracker who doesn't have free elections in his own country. No, if you never see me another time in your life, if I die in the morning, I'll die saying one thing: the ballot or the bullet, the ballot or the bullet (1966. 25–44).

It is evident in these lines that here we are faced with the voice of Malcolm X not the analyst but the prophetic one who is trying to urge people to stand up for reclaiming justice, liberty, right and their God-given human rights.

At his most analytic, Malcolm X conceived of theoretical engagement as a method to help suffering house-Negros to liberate themselves from crippling fear and to realize more of their creative potential. In this mode, he emphasized the importance of self-education at the start of political activism. At his most prophetic, Malcolm X's mission was to bring about a messianic age of peace and human solidarity, and he used Islam as a spiritual path for himself and those who were looking to become field-Negros. He viewed field-negro-symptoms as a partial rejection of oppressive or alienating authority. The field-negro leader's role was to help give birth to the revolutionary within the house-negro subject.

ACADEMIA AND THE PROPHETIC PERSPECTIVE

One of the serious questions before any social theorist or philosopher and even a theologian is the possibility of *prophetic engagement* in a *disenchanted world*. Of course, I am not arguing for the reemergence of prophets in the theological sense of the term as by prophetic quality I refer to the possibility of engaging the public square in a normative fashion rather than recreating indifferent strategies of being and living in all spheres of human life. The key to understand the question of disenchantment is rationalization which in general sense refers to the opposite of understanding the reality through mystery and magic, i.e. what Weber considers as the fate of our times which *"is characterized by rationalization and intellectualization and, above all, by the disenchantment of the world"* (Koshul, 2005. 11). In other words, how could one speak of individual responsibility in the face of a collective normative void? This is to argue that modern academia is based on the idea that there are " no mysterious incalculable forces that come into play, but rather that one can, in principle, master all things by calculation" (Weber, 1946. 139). To put it differently, the prophetic quality seems to be at odds with the spirit of time and those who aspire to have the mantle of prophets may look ridiculously like Don Quixote , i.e. being out of step with colossal changes of life in contemporary world.

If we take structures as decisive in the constitution of self and society then we should admit that the prophetic engagement belongs to a bygone epoch and those who aspire to revive *chivalric sentiments* should be considered as schizophrenic personalities who are in dire need of medical attention. However, if we assume that agency is as important as structure then we may understand the concept of normalcy in a different fashion than we understand today. In other words, a world which is indifferent to responsibility then it cannot sustain itself as the very pillars of modernity is based on negation of tutelage and that is the alpha and omega of all responsibilities. This is to argue that the prophetic perspective may be at odds with the spirit of disciplinary academia but this should not be the criterion in judging all other forms of engaging with reality and all that matters to humanity. To put it otherwise, Malcolm X may not fit within the parameters of disciplinary academia but disciplinary academia is not the only form of academic lifestyle or epistemic form of intellectual significance. Structures could be sustained in a normative void but human beings cannot endure normlessness forever and if anomie is a state of ontological insecurity then the prophetic sentiment could be the antidote of the collective normative void which has enveloped humanity in a cash-nexus world. If you look at all the articles which were published on race relations in America or books which analyzed the black question in America prior to Malcolm X's public engagement it is evident that the *negrofragae* was addressed in a very eloquent academic fashion but something was missing. I think the missing link is the total picture which could be drawn by a prophetic spirit who could transform the ways in which one looks at the reality in its totality. I think this is how Malcolm comes across in his prophetic quality when he says:

> Don't be shocked when I say that I was in prison. You're still in prison. That's what America means—prison. Who can deny that this is true for the black man? No matter how high he rises, he never loses consciousness of the invisible bars which hem him in. We did not land on Plymouth Rock. It landed on us (1966. Preface).

He does not take empirical approach in demonstrating how quantitatively the salary of black workers have increased in farms around the country or how segregation policies have been improved since the abolition of slavery. Although he is attentive to the importance of empirical approaches but these approaches are significant if the "whole picture" is not lost in details. In other words, the prophetic voice in Malcolm X enabled him to raise the consciousness of the Black people in US and the world beyond in a colossal fashion. This is to argue that even the world has been disenchanted but if we realize that enchanting possibilities could come about through actions which are not confined within the bars of disenchanted institutions. This brings us to the question of alternative forms of academia which are not the prisons of Christ but the safe haven of prophetic voice.

PERSONAL SCHOLARLY NARRATIVE

How does Malcolm X use the method of *Personal Scholarly Narrative* in making theoretically significant points?

There are many different ways of how he has employed the PSN method in relating his critiques but one of those interesting points is the question of "media construction"—which occupies a very important place in contemporary sociological debates. Of course we should bear in mind that when Malcolm X was talking about the impact of media the world of media was not as complex as it is today but he seems to have foreseen 21st century mediatization of reality. Malcolm X used to enlighten his audience by giving numerous examples and through these examples he attempted to engage with public issues. In other words, he used personal issues and made them public concerns and this he achieved through what I call Personal Scholarly Narrative. Here I can give you an excellent example of how Malcolm engaged with the public through his personal problems. He narrates that I

> Was flying from Algiers to Geneva about three or four weeks ago, and seated beside me on the airplane were a couple of Americans, both white, one a male and the other a female. One was an interpreter who worked in Geneva for the United Nations, the other was a girl who worked in one of the embassies in some part of Algeria. We conversed for about forty or forty-five minutes and then the lady, who had been looking at my briefcase, said, May I ask you a personal question? And I said, Yes. Because they always do anyway. She said, What kind of last name do you have that begins with X? I said, That's it, X. So she said, X? Yes. Well, what is your first name? I said, Malcolm. So she waited for about ten minutes and then she said, You're not Malcolm X. And I said, yes, I'm Malcolm X. Why, what's the matter? And she said, Well, you're not what I was looking for. What she was looking for was what the newspapers, the press, had created. She was looking for the image that the press had created. Somebody with some horns, . . . about to kill all the white people—as if he could kill all of them, or as if he shouldn't. She was looking for someone who was a rabble-rouser, who couldn't even converse with people . . . , someone who was irrational. . . . I take time to point this out, because it shows

how skillfully someone can take a newspaper and build an image of someone so that before you even meet them, you'll run. You don't even want to hear what they have to say, you don't even know them, all you know is what the press has had to say, and the press is white. And when I say the press is white, I mean it is white. And it's dangerous (1966. 91–2).

In other words, the "politics of media" is a serious question which has been reflected upon by Malcolm X in a very critical fashion. This is to argue that the question of "reality" is deeply related to the politics of hermeneutics which one should not neglect in regard to media—as though media reflects reality in a "naked form." Malcolm X is of the opinion that reality is *re-presented* through media which is "white" (i.e. it is biased) and moreover it should be realized that media is a medium of oppression in any panoptican social system.

Epilogue

It is no secret that the human mind receives information in a very selective fashion as formation of human cognitive faculty is deeply intertwined with aspects of reality which are not always of cognitive natures. In other words, one of the most complex issues related to the world of humanity is the selective propensity of human mind which problematizes the myth of innocent concepts. For instance, the term sociological imagination was coined by C. Wright Mills in 1959 to describe a particular form of insight but the imaginative dimensions of Mills' concept were not heard by the community of disciplinary social sciences at all. On the contrary, it has become a cliché that C. Wright Mills attempted to describe the type of insight offered by "the discipline of sociology." In other words, the kind of imagination which Mills was talking about is tantamount to the disciplinary form of knowledge which has been institutionalized in the academic discipline of sociology. If this is how Mills intended by imagination in his sociological understanding then why did he disagree with Parsons who was conceptualizing sociology within the legitimate frames of academic social sciences? I think the problem is that we only hear what we want to hear. This is a general cognitive problem which is part and parcel of being human person. To put it differently, the root cause of this problem is related to the question of knowledge, i.e. how is knowledge conceptualized? What do we consider as knowledge? Are forms of knowledge possible? Is plurality of knowledge a myth or a reality? With the disciplinary form of knowledge academic human cognition has grown accustomed to one style of knowledge at the expense of all undisciplinary forms of epistemes. Once we realize that there are different models of knowledge then we may fathom figures of knowledge production in a different fashion. In other words, this brings us to the old question of pantheon of sociology or social theory which is always part of the identity of sociology as a form of knowledge. This is to argue that we need to debunk the myth of "identity of sociology" by clarifying that we have always forms of identities within sociological enterprise and these differing identities would never converge in a single meta-sociological identity which is sanctioned by the board of trustees who follow the mode of clerkish rationalité (Miri, 2014. 56).

This reminds me of an incident in Bristol while I was doing my doctorate research in England. During a meeting which I had with Professor Gregor McLennan, I asked him about whom he considers as a sociologist, i.e. in his view what qualities do qualify a thinker to be considered as a sociologist? His answer was brief but enlightening and worked for me as a leitmotif in the past twenty years. He argued a sociologist is someone who can focus on local issues but draw global or even universal conclusions in regard to social problems and quests of human life. If we take this working definition as our point of departure then we can see that Malcolm X qualifies as a highly acclaimed social theorist as he looked at "particular issues" which concerned the Black Community in USA by coining novel concepts such as House Negro and Field Negro—which are not necessarily and squarely confined to *Negrofragae*. On the contrary, his illustrative descriptions and enlightening explanations could be employed as highly imaginative frame of theorizing for issues and theories such as "assimilation," "integration," "acculturation," "socialization," "alienation," "actualization," and strategies for overcoming cultural westoxification or cultural schizophrenia and many other contemporary problematiques which are highlighted in alternative social science discourses.

How could concepts by Malcolm X be used in relation to Muslim Community? My interest in posing this question is anthropological, historical, political, and epistemological. As far as who the "we" refers to: it actually refers, ultimately, to *all* Muslims—at least everyone who self-identifies as "Muslim." I will clarify a little later as to why (and how) I can make such an apparently outlandish claim. More immediately, the "we" refers to all Muslims who are involved in the production, dissemination, as well as—but maybe at a lower register—the consumption of "Islam." Why do I say this? Firstly, and perhaps most importantly, because the complex matrix of traditions that we have to come to identify as "Islamic" were significantly, possibly irrevocably (whether directly or indirectly) transformed by colonial policies and practices and ways of knowing "the Orient." This point is not considered very radical from the point-of-view of postcolonial studies but it is worth noticing in relation to reading Malcolm X in novel fashions. The second reason I pose my provocation as to whether "we" are "house Muslims" or "field Muslims"—while deriving initially from the first reason—is because, as a subject of discussion, contestation, and refutation "Islam" (and what I have to say is not entirely separable from this fray, of course) is always already interpellated by disciplinary/eurocentric structures of power/knowledge. Those of us involved with/in the academy in any way surely experience this—perhaps acutely.

In a Foucaultian fashion, it could be argued that knowledge—and here I am pointing to the production of knowledge "about Islam," and speaking "for Islam" as well as "on behalf of Muslims"—is not separable from the "force relations" (the system/s of relations overseen by power, *by* and *through* which various expressions are emphasized, curtailed, contained, refined, elided) in which such a production and dissemination and consumption of "Islam" occurs.

Thus, Malcolm X's sociological concepts could be applied to the Muslim question or even intellectual traditions in the *restern* contexts by asking to what extent they are "house intellectuals" and to what extent they are "filed intellectuals" or "house Muslims," and to what extent they are "field Muslims." What I would like to suggest is that probably the vast majority of Muslims, as far as their relationship to power/knowledge—given colonialism and the virtual ubiquity of its reconfiguring of "Islam"—fall into the category of "field Muslims." A significant portion of "Muslims" in the West, on the other hand—at least those of them who have to negotiate (consciously and unconsciously) where what is called "Islam" may be located within the measure of "Good Muslim vs. Bad Muslim"/"Moderate vs. Extremist"—which is of course a measure placed from without; and this is in addition to the "internal" discussions as to what constitutes "a good Muslim"—are probably a mixture of the two ("house Muslim" and "field Muslim"), as it was suggested above.

Of course, this is only one example of how Malcolm X's concepts could be employed in problematizing significant social questions provided we do not get trapped in disciplinary forms of imagination. In other words, we need to dare to imagine wild dreams and these wildest dreams could only become reality if we embark on untrodden ways or as the unknown poet says *One must dwell among the untrodden ways Beside the springs of Doves.* This is to argue that concept-formation is a necessary step in creation of alternative modes of knowledge and Malcolm X is one of the most important social theorists who could assist us in this tumultuous path to self-recovery in the 21st century.

References

Adams, J. T. *The Epic of America*. Little, Brown and Company in Boston, 1931.

Asad, Talal. *Formations of the Secular: Christianity, Islam, and Modernity*. Palo Alto, CA: Stanford University Press, 2003.

Bowie, Andrew. *Aesthetics and Subjectivity: From Kant to Nietzsche*. Manchester: Manchester University Press, 1990.

Byrd, D. J. "Marable Manning; Malcolm X: A Life of Reinvention" *Islamic Perspective*, Vol. 6, 2011, pp. 245-58.

Dallmayr, Winfried R. *Twilight of Subjectivity: Contributions to a Post-Individualist Theory Politics*. Amherst, MA: University of Massachusetts Press, 1981.

Dostoevsky, M. F. *The Brothers Karamazov*. Translated into Persian by Moshfegh Hamedani. Published at Badraqeh Javidan, Tehran, 2009.

Du Bois, W. E. B. *Black Reconstruction: An essay toward a history of the part which black folk played in the attempt to reconstruct democracy in America, 1860-1880*. New York, Harcourt, Brace and Company, 1935.

Ellis, C. & Flaherty, M. (1992). *Investigating Subjectivity: Research on Lived Experience*. Newbury Park, CA: Sage, 1992.

Farrell, Frank B. Farrell. *Subjectivity, Realism, and Postmodernism: The Recovery of the World in Recent Philosophy*. New York: Cambridge University Press, 1994.

Fromm, E. *The Sane Society*. Owl Books; New York, 1955.

Freud, S. Instincts and their Vicissitudes. *Standard Edition of the Complete Psychological Works of Sigmund Freud*, Vol. 14, 1957, pp. 111-140. J. Strachey (Trans. & Gen. Ed.) in collaboration with A. Freud, assisted by A. Strachey & A. Tyson. London: Hogarth Press, 1915.

Hill, A. *How to Draw*. Pan Books, 1963.

Koshul, Basit Bilal. *The postmodern significance of Max Weber's legacy: disenchanting disenchantment*. Macmillan, 2005.

Lauer, Q. *The Triumph of Subjectivity: An Introduction to Transcendental Phenomenology.* Fordham University Press, 1958.

Mahmood Saba. *Politics of Piety: The Islamic Revival and the Feminist Subject.* Princeton, NJ: Princeton University Press, 2005.

Mahmood Saba. "Religious Reason and Secular Affect: An Incommensurable Divide?" *Critical Inquiry* 2009; 35: 836-862.

Miri, S. J. *Beyond Eurocentrism: Probing into Epistemological Endeavors of Allama Jafari.* London: London Academy of Iranian Studies Press, 2014.

Nicholas, Pope. "Dum Diversas (English Translation)," *Unam Sanctam Catholicam*, February 27, 2011. Retrieved on 14 August 2014.

Rabaka, R. "Malcolm X and/as Critical Theory: Philosophy, Radical Politics, and the African American Search for Social Justice", *Journal of Black Studies*, Vol. 33, No. 2, November 2002, 145-165.

Rojas, C. An. A. "1968 as a turning point in historical thinking: Changes in western historiography" *Hisotória, Sao Paulo*, 23 (1-2): 2004, pp. 197-218.

Steiner, G. Heidegger. The Harvester Press Limited, Sussex, 1978.

Tyler, S. A. *The Said and the Unsaid: Mind, Meaning and Culture.* New York: Academic Press, 1978.

Underhill, James W. *Ethnolinguistics and Cultural Concepts: Truth, love, hate & war.* Cambridge: Cambridge University Press, 2012.

Warnock, M. Existentialism. Oxford University Press, Oxford, 1970.

Weber, Max. *From Max Weber: Essays in Sociology.* Translated and edited by H. H. Gerth and C. Wright Mills. New York: Oxford University Press, 1946.

X, Malcolm. *Malcolm X Speaks.* New York: Grove Press, 1966.

Žižek, S. Demanding the Impossible. Ed. Yong-June Park. Cambridge, UK: Polity Press, 2013.

www.ingramcontent.com/pod-product-compliance
Lightning Source LLC
Chambersburg PA
CBHW020753230426

43665CB00009B/581